Memories
of Steam

Memories *of* Steam

RELIVING THE GOLDEN AGE OF BRITAIN'S RAILWAYS

TOM QUINN

PICTURES SELECTED AND
DESCRIBED BY JULIAN HOLLAND

D&C
David and Charles

A DAVID & CHARLES BOOK
Copyright © David & Charles Limited 2008

David & Charles is an imprint of F&W Media International, Ltd
Brunel House, Forde Close, Newton Abbot, TQ12 4PU, UK

F&W Media International, Ltd is a subsidiary of F+W Media, Inc
10151 Carver Road, Suite #200, Blue Ash, OH 45242, USA

First published in the UK in 2008
Reprinted with corrections in 2008, 2009 (twice)
This paperback edition first published in 2010

Text copyright © Tom Quinn 2008
Photographs copyright © see page 250

ISBN-13: 978-0-7153-2957-3
ISBN-10: 0-7153-2957-X

Printed in China by RR Donnelley
for David & Charles
Brunel House, Newton Abbot, Devon

Head of Publishing: Alison Myer
Commissioning Editor: Neil Baber
Editorial Manager: Emily Pitcher
Assistant Editor: Sarah Wedlake
Art Editor: Sarah Clark
Picture Researcher and Captions: Julian Holland
Project Editor: James Loader
Production Controller: Beverley Richardson

F+W Media publishes high-quality books on a wide range
of subjects.
For more great book ideas visit: www. thehobbywarehouse.co.uk

CONTENTS

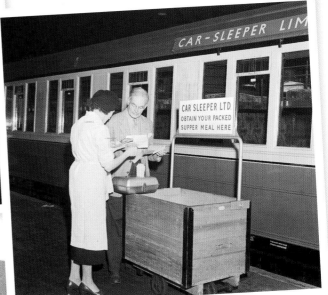

Introduction

When the last steam trains vanished in the 1960s from all but a few preserved railways, the travelling public, as well as drivers, firemen, porters and guards, probably imagined they were about to enter a brave new world of cleaner, brighter, more efficient travel. This after all was an era during which we embraced all things modern – from rock and roll to bright plastic furniture. It was an era during which, for example, auction houses such as Sotheby's virtually stopped organizing sales of Victorian paintings and furniture because there was no demand. In our houses we threw out panelled doors and marble fireplaces in a ruthless break with the past that now seems almost incomprehensible.

But like all brave new worlds this one never quite matched expectations; on the railways drivers might have enjoyed their cleaner and more comfortable cabs, but they quickly realized that the new world had taken away far more than it gave. The special quality of their work – the romance if you like – had vanished; instead of becoming much admired champions of hi-tech they had declined into mere technicians and, moreover, technicians who needed little training to do a job that, in the steam era, had taken a decade or more to learn.

In the wider world the vastly evocative smells and noises of steam travel were quickly missed, perhaps partly because railway travel was the first mass transport system that felt democratic. It took millions of ordinary people on journeys that would never have happened for them in the days when travel was powered, at best, by the horse. A century and more of travel glamour and excitement could not be erased overnight and no sooner had we lost the vast edifice of steam than we wanted it back. We wanted fire and steam to accompany our journeys between the great Victorian cities that spawned the railways in the first place, and we wanted the wonder and magic of rattling, steam-powered excursions through a still unspoilt countryside.

Of course we can still enjoy the sights and sounds and smells of the steam era through numerous preserved railways – some, such as the Watercress Line in Hampshire, provide an almost uncannily accurate recreation of the past – but there is nothing now to remind us of the realities of a time when the whole rail system was driven by steam. Nothing, that is, except the memories of those who knew that vanished world from the inside.

Despite the passage of more than four decades since the last mainline steam services ended, millions of men and women still recall that lost age with great fondness; and although their numbers are rapidly dwindling, there are still many railway workers who remember their lives as guards, drivers, firemen, porters and signalmen in those far-off days.

This book is based on lengthy interviews with dozens of passengers and railway workers whose memories date back to the 1930s and in some cases to a time when the death of Queen Victoria was a recent event. In the early 1980s I began recording the memories of retired railwaymen and women. These interviews were mostly with those born around 1900 or a little earlier. All these 'early' interviewees are now dead, but over the years since the 1980s I have recorded the memories of many other, younger people, including many who recall that fascinating transition period when, with the end of steam already in sight, locomotives were still being built in one region while they were being phased out in another.

Other interviewees remember the shock of the Beeching Cuts, the hardships of wartime travel, the gloom and austerity of the 1950s, the essentially Victorian nature of much of the 1920s and 1930s railway infrastructure.

My store of interviews adds up to perhaps a million and more words – words that conjure an intimate picture of steam travel as it really was. This book is, if you like, a distillation of those million words and an attempt to recreate the past through the lives and memories of people who were there. It is also perhaps a tribute to a transport system that changed forever the way we live.

AT THE STATION

The great London termini were the pride of the big four railway companies – reflected in their sheer size and in the quality of their architecture – but smaller stations and rural halts also played a part in the journeys of many during the steam era.

Station Approach

'... the station could be very quiet ... in fact I pretty much knew all the passengers'

The grand sweep of the entrance road to St Pancras Station in London – not to mention the magnificent Gothic railway hotel that soars above it – is a reminder of the style and grandeur of early railway travel. Here the carriages of the upper classes swept in from their houses in Kensington and Belgravia.

Arriving in droves in August with three or four carriages filled with servants, luggage and shooting and fishing equipment, they were bound for the sleeper to Scotland's grouse moors. Along the Marylebone Road serving four of the great London termini – Euston, King's Cross, St Pancras and Marylebone – horse-drawn omnibuses and hansom cabs plied their trade, bringing the less well-off from the suburbs.

In the countryside it was very different. Here, smaller stations and halts were often built some way from the village centre, but a walk or cycle of a mile or more was hardly an inconvenience to a community that had never before enjoyed public transport of any kind. A 20-minute walk and cheap tickets meant the pleasure of an easy outing to the town or the seaside.

Goods arrived at stations in the early days by horse and cart, but stations, however small, kept their own horses and carts too, for shunting work and for moving goods and passengers into the nearest town.

Sussex stationmaster Stan Smith, born in 1921 into a family of railway workers (his grandfather was at work in the mid-1800s), said:

The railway cart is a thing few people remember today. Most stations, however small, had at least one cart, because when the parcels arrived by train they had to be delivered round the town and we used a horse and cart to do it. Bigger stations would have had far more carts and in the rush of a busy day they would all have been in use, carrying goods and luggage from the carriages and wagons that pulled up at the station, but also moving goods and luggage from the trains to waiting vehicles. In many areas station horses and carts lasted well into the motor transport era.

■ PREVIOUS PAGE: A BUSY SCENE ON PLATFORM 1 AT PADDINGTON STATION IN THE 1950S.

■ A LINE OF TAXI CABS OUTSIDE WATERLOO STATION IN LONDON, MAY 1934.

Many small stations were also like post offices, selling stamps and collecting parcels, which is why Stan's grandfather managed to combine the roles of stationmaster and postmaster.

He was always busy meeting important people when they arrived at the station, but also checking that all passengers were properly treated and that arrivals and departures went smoothly. As postmaster he made sure all parcels arriving were loaded on to the station cart and taken carefully round the town.

Station porter Tom Jales remembered how horses were still used for station work long after cars had become commonplace:

Even in the 1930s I would be passed by quite a bit of horse-drawn traffic, much of it carrying loads to the station. Opposite my house was a road haulier who only had horses – he got a lot of work from the railways.

■ WEST RUNTON STATION BOARD ON THE MIDLAND AND GREAT NORTHERN JOINT RAILWAY.

■ AN UN-REBUILT BULLEID 'BATTLE OF BRITAIN' CLASS 4-6-2 SHUTS OFF STEAM FOR A SPEED RESTRICTION WHILE WORKING A VICTORIA TO RAMSGATE TRAIN AT CHESTFIELD & SWALECLIFFE HALT NEAR WHITSTABLE.

Important local firms didn't drop their goods off in the normal way due to a special relationship with the local station, as stationmaster Rod Lock recalled:

At East Winch in Norfolk back in the 1930s and 1940s, much of the freight was agricultural produce, particularly grain. Our local firm supplied so much that they had a private siding – they didn't pay much but day in and day out their grain was forwarded at the rate of about two or three wagonloads a day. And if you multiply that by all the thousands of tiny rural stations up and down the country doing similar levels of business you can see why the railways could survive in small, out-of-the-way places.

We had our regular passengers, too, although the station could be very quiet even at the weekends in summer – in fact I pretty much knew all the passengers. Many cycled to the station or walked and I never remember their bikes being locked up – no one would have thought that a bike left at a little country station might be stolen and of course they never were!

DUNCHURCH PLUMS
Passengers who arrived or departed from the pretty station of Dunchurch during late summer and early autumn in the 1940s and 1950s were as likely as not to be given a handful of plums by the stationmaster, who collected the fruit in buckets from the trees that grew at the station. He clearly felt that railway plums were not to be squandered!

■ AN ATTRACTIVE, CHALET-STYLE STATION BUILDING AND PROFUSION OF FLOWERS ADD TO THE APPEAL OF THIS SMALL HIGHLAND STATION, ON THE BRANCHLINE NEAR LOCH LOMOND. A NORTH BRITISH CLASS C15 4-4-2T STANDS AT THE PLATFORM.

■ THE CLOCK AT MALVERN STATION STANDS AMID HANGING BASKETS AND THE ORNATE TRACERY OF THE DECORATED COLUMN SUPPORTS FOR THE PLATFORM CANOPIES.

STATION PRIDE

While the big termini impressed with the grandeur of their architecture, smaller stations vied with each other in producing attractive and neatly kept environments – simply to stand on a station platform was regarded as a pleasure in itself.

■ To this day Dolau Station on the Central Wales Line is renowned for its floral displays.

■ Great Western Railway station signs were often set off by flower beds, as at Kingham Station, shown here.

Restaurants and Waiting Rooms

By all accounts the earliest railways were pretty uncomfortable from a passenger's point of view, with open trucks, poor suspension and hard benches to sit on. But the railway entrepreneurs quickly realized that the way to make this extraordinary new means of transport really successful was to make your passengers comfortable. Open trucks were soon replaced and waiting rooms began to appear on station platforms across the country. The best – for First Class passengers – had fireplaces and comfortable chairs and must have been a godsend in winter. There were also Second (uncomfortable) and Third (very uncomfortable) Class waiting rooms and even waiting rooms reserved for women.

At Paddington we know that in 1838 the Great Western Railway appointed its very first female employee, Mary Coulsell, as a full-time attendant in the ladies' waiting room, which was fitted with plenty of glass so that nothing untoward could happen out of sight of the public!

Stations quickly attracted booksellers, newsagents, restaurants and cafés. Tea shops and small restaurants were a feature of the earliest railway. Though they were eventually taken over by British Railways they were originally franchises sold to the highest bidder. Cafés and restaurants were often small poky affairs, but in London and other large cities they were built on a grand scale.

Sheila Kehoe, who lived in Paddington for 60 years, remembered one station tea shop that was clearly a cut above the rest:

We used to get to Marylebone station early deliberately to have tea in the tea shop before catching our train to the country. Originally the tea shop had a lovely Edwardian feel to it and although it was updated over the years it was always comfortable – at least until the British Rail era – and in the early days surprisingly quiet. They brought in cakes from local shops, but made their own sandwiches.

In fact the early railways provided a sudden new and extensive range of career opportunities for women. We don't know quite how many women were employed at the big restaurants at mainline stations but all the indications are that the numbers were high – they were employed in the kitchens, of course, but also as waitresses, clerks and, in the hotels, as chambermaids.

So much a part of life did the first refreshment rooms become that they were even satirized in *Punch* magazine, where the caricaturist Richard Doyle included a sketch of the refreshment room at Swindon in his satire on the manners and customs of the English published in 1849.

A century and more later restaurants were still vital to the smooth running of most big stations and many smaller ones. Waiting rooms remained important too.

■ MANY RAILWAY RESTAURANTS OFFERED GOOD FOOD AND STYLISH SERVICE, AS AT MANCHESTER LONDON ROAD STATION, C.1956.

Signalman George Case, at work in the 1940s, recalled a particularly unusual waiting room:

The signals training school at Hatfield was established in a former royal waiting room on one of the platforms and the story of how it came to be there provides an interesting glimpse of the relationship between railways and royalty in former times.

Queen Victoria had visited Hatfield often as it is the nearest station to Hatfield House, home of the Cecils. In order to accommodate the queen in the style to which she had long been accustomed, the platforms at Hatfield were built staggered – in other words they were built in such a way that they do not face each other across the tracks in the normal way. When the royal train stopped at the station the staggered platforms meant there was no chance that another train could stop opposite the Royal train. Thus the queen avoided the risk of being ogled by her subjects.

The Hatfield royal waiting room was kept in perfect order, but unused, until 1943. It had a lovely big fireplace, carpets and pictures and a table. In 1943 the war persuaded officials that they'd better make some use of it. And so it became a signals school for young men like me.

Perhaps the last word should go to the great railway engineer Brunel. He complained loudly about the quality of the coffee at the refreshment room he himself designed at Swindon station, but before the era of dining cars, station restaurants had to be big, efficient and very fast. The reason? Well, on what is now the North Eastern line, expresses making their way from London to Scotland were scheduled to stop at York, Normanton and Preston so that passengers could eat and drink – but with each stop just lasting 20 to 30 minutes both staff and customers had to be quick!

■ A HAPPY FAMILY SCENE AT BUILTH ROAD (LOW LEVEL) REFRESHMENT ROOM ON 24 AUGUST 1962.

■ THE BRITISH RAILWAYS TRAVEL CENTRE AT SLOUGH IN THE EARLY 1960S.

Railway Hotels

The extent to which the railways were once considered the height of fashionable travel can be judged by the magnificence of station hotels. Many very beautiful examples were destroyed in the 1960s along with the stations themselves – most famously Euston – but many survived to enjoy a distinct revival in their popularity. The Midland Grand Hotel, designed by the great Sir George Gilbert Scott and opened in 1873 at St Pancras, escaped demolition by a hair's breadth but has now been restored and is in use once again as a hotel after years of neglect.

But at the other end of the country, in Perth, the station hotel was just as important as it was in London. The Perth Station Hotel – which survives to this day – was a place of warmth and comfort and sheer pleasure, as William Acworth recalled in the early 20th century:

The passenger who is kept waiting at Perth Station Hotel must admit that there is not much fault to be found with the accommodation there provided for him. Even the dogs are not forgotten and, after their hot night in the train, should enjoy their roomy kennels with fresh water and clean straw. For their masters there are comfortable dressing rooms with baths all complete, while downstairs the breakfast, with its never-ending relays of fresh Tay salmon, can fairly challenge comparison with the famous bouillabaisse of the Marseilles buffet.

■ THE HOTEL GREAT CENTRAL WAS OPENED IN 1899 TO COINCIDE WITH THE COMPLETION OF BRITAIN'S LAST MAIN LINE FROM NOTTINGHAM TO LONDON MARYLEBONE. ONE OF THE GRANDEST OF LONDON'S RAILWAY HOTELS, IT IS NOW KNOWN AS THE LANDMARK LONDON.

The early railway companies invested in hotels because they were money-spinners. Journey times, though incomparably better than journey times by stage coach, were still long and exhausting – a whole day to reach Aberdeen from London for example – and before on-train lavatories and dining cars travellers were grateful for regular stops and the chance perhaps to break their journey in a luxurious hotel. That no doubt explains why all the major provincial cities of England had railway hotels by 1900.

■ THE GREAT EASTERN RAILWAY'S FLAGSHIP HOTEL (LEFT) WAS AT LIVERPOOL STREET IN LONDON. THE GLASGOW & SOUTH WESTERN RAILWAY'S HOTEL AT TURNBERRY (RIGHT) WAS A FAVOURITE HAUNT OF GOLFERS.

BRUNEL'S COMPLAINT

While working on the Great Western Railway in the 1840s Brunel wrote to the owner of the Swindon Railway Hotel: 'Dear Sir, I assure you Mr Player was wrong in supposing that I thought you purchased inferior coffee. I thought I said to him that I was surprised you should buy such bad roasted corn. I did not believe you had such a thing as coffee in the place. I am sure I never tasted any. I have long ceased to make complaints at Swindon. I avoid taking anything there when I can help it.'

J.W. Robertson Scott, who travelled widely by train, recalled the experience of staying in several railway hotels just after the Great War:

It is difficult now to comprehend the splendour and luxury of railway hotels in that golden era after 1918. Railway travel then was fashionable and not just a means to get from A to B and the hotels reflected this – stations at the London termini were always richly appointed, with a great deal of marble imported from across the world. Entrance halls were lofty, pillared and magnificent and vast restaurants served the finest food amidst rich velvety Victorian wallpapers, potted palms and beautifully made mahogany tables and chairs and sideboards. Labour was cheap at that time, too, and you could hardly walk a few feet in a railway hotel without a member of staff asking if they could help you in some way. In many ways the atmosphere the railway owners tried to create in their hotels was the atmosphere of the English country house: grand, luxurious, imposing and staffed by an army of low-paid servants. Of course they were shrewd in this because many of the wealthiest travellers in those days wanted to stay where standards were as high as they were at home and the newly emerging rich loved to ape the lifestyle of old money.

By the time British Rail was created in January 1948 there were 54 railway hotels but already by this period many were struggling to survive, as the motor car began to change forever the habits of the travelling public.

On the Platform

In the days of steam, stations in rural areas competed to be the prettiest or tidiest station. Flower beds were planted, timberwork kept tidy and regularly painted, platforms swept every day; brass, lamps and buckets polished. In the big cities, stations were designed to reflect the pride of the local railway company; their architecture was grand and decorative, reaching a peak of sophistication in the great London termini, but there was a charm, too, in the platform furniture and architecture of even the smallest rural station.

COMPENSATION CULTURE

In the 1890s a woman sued the Southern Region railway company for injuries sustained when she slipped on the platform. At the court case a rail official was convinced he'd seen the woman before, so set off to do some detective work. He discovered that this was the fourth claim brought against the company by the woman – on one occasion she'd been awarded a large sum as a result of total and permanent paralysis! Back in court the judge dismissed the case and told her that if he saw her in court again he would jail her.

■ MINERS WAITING FOR THE AFTERNOON SPECIAL, AN LMS DESIGNED FAIRBURN 2-6-4T, AT THE CHISLET COLLIERY HALT ON THE KENT COALFIELD.

Platforms were also the proving ground for young railway enthusiasts. Today it seems bizarre that anyone should want to buy a platform ticket, a ticket that entitled you to be on the platform but not travel, but in earlier days being on the platform was a pleasure in itself; a pleasure often unrelated to the pleasure of travelling, as the young Richard Hardy, growing up in the 1930s, remembered:

The great Central engines, passing through Amersham, really hooked me. I was on the platform every day of the holidays when I came home from school at Marlborough. I got to know all the railway staff – they were incredibly friendly. Eventually the footplate men knew me, too, and I was given trips to Rickmansworth and Wendover. Can you imagine that now? Not likely.

'I got to know all the railway staff – they were incredibly friendly'

'Quick as a flash he leapt over, picked up the poodle dropping and put it in his pocket'

Signalman George Case, who started work aged 14 in 1940, remembered just how keen the management was to keep the platforms spotless, especially under certain circumstances, as he explained:

I remember particularly Chitty Mason, who kept the platforms tidy at King's Cross. One day Princess Margaret had just arrived and was about to get off her train when Chitty spotted a poodle using the red carpet in an unmentionable fashion outside her carriage. Quick as a flash he leapt over, picked up the poodle dropping and put it in his pocket. He walked calmly over to me and simply said, 'That was a near miss, guv.'

■ SETTING OFF FOR AN OUTING FROM A TYPICALLY RUGGED NORTHERN STATION.

Porter Tom Jales, who was born in 1913, remembered how busy the platforms could be:

My other jobs in those early days before the war were sweeping the platform every day and unloading the milk – you quickly got the knack of rolling two great churns along the platform to the carts waiting outside the station.

Normally, in one delivery we'd have about a hundred churns to roll – a hell of a back-breaking job, but there were several porters and we enjoyed doing it together.

Tom also recalled trains arriving where there were two platforms for the one train:

If a train stopped at one particular platform at Finsbury Park a porter was needed on both sides of the train, because it was a single track and passengers could get on and off on both sides.

Once the train was due to depart the leading or senior porter would shout over the top of the train, 'Are you all right there?' If you shouted 'Yes' in reply, he'd wave his flag, then you'd wave yours and they'd be off.

And the platforms themselves had to be spotless, as another trainee porter, Sid Daniels, recalled:

We had an inspector who was famous for walking along shouting, 'You know your duty!' when we were sweeping the long platforms. Then he'd shout, 'I don't want to make you do it again!', which was usually a sure sign that he had every intention of making us do it again!

Harry Horn's first job was as a lamp boy at Starcross in Devon. At a time when all platform illumination was by oil this was an important position. It was also virtually full time, as the old primitive one-wick lamps had to be trimmed and attended to every day. In Norfolk Rod Lock

recalled the importance of station appearance and particularly the platforms:

My first boss was a stationmaster of the old school, formally dressed and always carrying himself with great dignity. He was also very proud of his work.

He showed me all the little extra jobs that improved the station, like putting posters up regularly and keeping the platforms and station garden looking tidy. In those days cash prizes were often given for the best-kept station and we always hoped to win, though we never did.

PLATFORM FACTS

The longest station platform in England can be found at Gloucester. It's 602.6m long – around six times longer than a football pitch.

The world's largest station is Grand Central in New York, with a huge number of platforms – 44 in total.

The longest station seat in the world is on a platform at Scarborough Station. It is a lengthy 139m long.

■ A BUSY SCENE ON PLATFORM 7 AT PADDINGTON STATION IN THE 1950S.A

PLATFORM CONCESSIONS

Passengers likely to be in their seat for an hour or two were always going to be a ready market for anyone who could provide something to read on the journey or a quick drink or snack on the platform. WH Smith took advantage of the opportunity, opening its first concession at Euston in 1848 and quickly expanding to all parts of the country. John Menzies had similar dominance in Scotland.

■ WYMAN & SONS NEWSAGENTS STAND ON PLATFORMS 12 AND 13 AT EUSTON STATION, C.1908.

■ A GREAT WESTERN RAILWAY REFRESHMENT TROLLEY AT PADDINGTON STATION, C.1910.

■ WH SMITH NEWSPAPER AND CONFECTIONERY KIOSK AT ORPINGTON STATION ON THE SOUTHERN REGION.

■ WH SMITH MAGAZINE STALL BY THE ANGLO-SCOTTISH CAR CARRIER TRAIN IN MAY 1960.

■ OFFICIAL LONDON & NORTH WESTERN RAILWAY PHOTOGRAPH SHOWING A BOY SELLING NEWSPAPERS AT HOLYHEAD STATION, C.1905.

'... when you went to buy a railway ticket it was still something special because it cost a lot'

At the Ticket Barrier

Today's railway tends to rely on spot checks to make sure fare dodgers are caught and that passengers have bought the appropriate ticket for their journey. Tickets can be bought at machines, there are electronic barriers and human contact can seem quite minimal. In the steam era, by contrast, tickets were always issued by staff and you were checked on to the platform and off it at the end of your journey by the ticket collector. Your ticket would also be checked at least once by the guard on the train.

Rose Plummer recalled buying tickets at King's Cross station:
Well, my memory is that when you went to buy a railway ticket it was still something quite special because it cost a lot. I'm pretty sure it was more expensive before the war – even if you travelled Third Class – than it is in real terms today. My dad told me that in the early days of the railway, tokens were issued but we got thick card tickets that were always being punched by the train guard to make sure you didn't use them again. I remember your ticket might be checked several times on one journey – it definitely would be if you changed trains a few times.

> ## TOP FARE
> In November 2004 a used railway ticket for a seven-mile journey from Poole to Wimbourne in Dorset sold at auction for an astounding £2,352. The Second Class ticket, issued on 8 September 1863, was predicted to reach around £100 but was snapped up for 23 times the expected amount. The highest bidder, the anonymous widow of a railway enthusiast from Kent, set the world record for a used railway ticket.

Sheila Kehoe agreed:

In small country stations you might still find that the man in the ticket booth would sell you a ticket and it would then be punched by the ticket man at the barrier, which I suppose would be called overmanning these days. I seem to recall, however, that the ticket man also did portering and other work. In their smart suits – always three-piece serge and with a cap always on their heads – railway staff in the 1940s and 1950s were figures of authority, especially to the young. You would no more be rude or cheeky to a stationmaster or porter than to a policeman, because you assumed the consequences would be the same – you'd be in a lot of trouble. I think today people worry much less about figures of authority or even authority in general. I can't remember any cases of fare dodging either – although I do remember a porter chasing a man along the platform because he'd bought the wrong ticket and it was the booking clerk's fault. They even kept the train waiting a minute or two for him!

Tom Shackle thought it was a watertight system but an expensive one.:

The old railway put a lot of effort into avoiding loss of income through fare dodging but labour was very cheap in the old days – particularly before the war. Today it would cost so much more to employ extra staff that the savings in fares collected from fare dodgers wouldn't be anywhere near enough to cover the cost of the number of people you'd need to employ to make it work. And don't let anyone tell you that ticket buying is more complicated today than it was before nationalization – it was very complicated if your journey was complicated, just as it is today, although of course all the SuperSavers and other gimmicks didn't exist.

Fixtures and Fittings

An early account of how a station should be organized reveals a great deal about the pride early station builders had in what they were trying to create – the idea was clearly to provide an aesthetically pleasing environment for the passenger rather than a simple point of arrival or departure.

'... at important stations for a moderate charge passengers could even wash and dress after a journey'

Gordon Gill remembered how his father, a Birmingham railway architect, described the ideal station:

At more important stations there were waiting rooms for First, Second and Third Class passengers, with separate ladies' rooms, separate offices for the stationmaster and the telegraph clerks, rooms for left luggage, a lamp room, a place for heating water for foot warmers, up-and-down parcels offices, refreshment rooms with kitchen, scullery and accommodation for the attendants of the refreshment room, and ample WC and urinal accommodation. A great boon to travellers at important stations was a lavatory where for a moderate charge passengers could even wash and dress after a journey.

A house – or in the case of large stations, two houses – was provided above the station buildings, in which the stationmaster and the official next in command could live. The house was usually designed not to connect directly with the booking offices, as it was felt that if it was too easy to get from the one to the other the result might be 'inattention to duty'. Railway companies often provided houses for their stationmasters, porters, platelayers and signalmen, so a local railway became something of a community.

■ THE GREAT EASTERN RAILWAY'S CREST (ABOVE) AT LIVERPOOL STREET STATION IN LONDON.

■ A TYPICAL GREAT WESTERN RAILWAY PLATFORM SEAT (LEFT), THIS ONE CLEARLY PIECED TOGETHER FROM MORE THAN ONE ORIGINAL — THE DESIGN OF THE LOGOS ON THE CAST IRON SUPPORTS REFLECTING TWO DIFFERENT ERAS OF GWR.

■ THE ZERO MILEPOST AT YORK STATION (RIGHT) MARKS THE STARTING POINT FOR MANY EARLY RAILWAY COMPANIES.

Billy Westall recalled how carefully station architecture was cared for:

If you look at the pillars that support the canopy above any country railway station you will see elaborate decorative ironwork; and the buildings will often have rubbed brickwork, elaborate iron brackets for platform furniture – seats, clock supports, destination boards. The early railway architects hated the idea that they were building a purely functional station – they wanted something that was pleasing to the eye as well as useful, which is why even humble weather-boarded station buildings in remote out-of-the-way places were always simple but attractive, with well-made sash windows, decorative chimneys and so on. Even the fire buckets hanging on the walls were often painted bright colours.

In the big cities, of course, stations like Euston, St Pancras and Paddington involved architectural features that were the marvel of the age – the roof at Paddington when built had the biggest span of any similar roof in the world. The Grand Midland Hotel, at St Pancras in London – recently restored and re-opened – was and is a masterpiece of High Gothic architecture. Every detail of the bedrooms, halls, staircases and public areas was meant to dazzle and amaze, with a mass of carvings, ornate woodwork, stained glass and so on.

'The early railway architects hated the idea that they were building a purely functional station'

■ WROUGHT IRON PLATFORM GATES AT LONDON'S VICTORIA STATION GAVE A SENSE OF CONSEQUENCE TO PASSENGERS STARTING ON THEIR JOURNEY TO EAST GRINSTEAD.

■ THE STATION CLOCK AT BOLTON STATION IN THE 1950S PROMOTED THE TOWN'S LOCAL NEWSPAPER.

Down in the West Country Harry Horn recalled the fixtures and fittings of a small country station:

Even the old oil lamps that I tended as a boy were beautifully made; so were the benches on the platforms, and the ticket office was a splendid piece of joinery. Up in London and Birmingham we knew that ticket offices and waiting rooms were often marvels of brass, marble and glass. It made you proud to be part of it.

At the Station **37**

STATIONS, BUT NO TRAINS

Line closures throughout the history of the railways, most notably following the Beeching cuts of the 1960s, left station buildings large and small in search of a new purpose. Many of the smaller rural stations have been converted into private homes and others are now museums, shops or even, as shown here, fire stations.

- THE FORMER STATION BUILDING AT HULME END ON THE LEEK & MANIFOLD VALLEY LIGHT RAILWAY NOW SERVES AS A VISITOR CENTRE FOR THE MANIFOLD WAY FOOTPATH AND CYCLEWAY.

- BARNSTAPLE TOWN STATION, WHICH SERVED THE BARNSTAPLE TO ILFRACOMBE LINE AND WAS ALSO THE TERMINUS OF THE NARROW GAUGE LYNTON & BARNSTAPLE RAILWAY UNTIL 1935, IS NOW USED AS A SCHOOL.

- THE NORTHERN SCOTTISH SPA TOWN OF STRATHPEFFER ONCE HAD ITS OWN BRANCH LINE FROM DINGWALL (ABOVE). THIS CLOSED IN 1946 AND THE STATION BUILDING IS NOW A SHOPPING MALL.

- KIRKMICHAEL STATION (FAR LEFT), ON THE ST JOHN'S TO RAMSEY LINE OF THE ISLE OF MAN RAILWAYS, CLOSED IN 1968. THE BUILDING IS NOW USED AS A FIRE STATION.

- MANCHESTER CENTRAL STATION (LEFT) CLOSED IN 1969. THE TRAIN SHED, WHICH SPANS 210FT AND IS 550FT LONG AND 90FT HIGH, NOW HOUSES A CONFERENCE AND EXHIBITION CENTRE KNOWN AS THE GMEX CENTRE.

TRAVELLING BY TRAIN

Any journey by steam train, particularly before World War II, was an adventure for passengers – for the rich it was an adventure combined with luxury living.

Travelling in Different Styles

The Edwardian era is generally considered the great age of the train. Motor cars and aeroplanes were hardly thought of and the wealthy were looked after in some style.

They enjoyed luxurious carriages and attentive staff, while Third and Second Class carriages were decidedly less salubrious, as Tom Shackle remembered:

The corridors and every bit of the Third Class compartments were floored with brown lino. First Class was furnished with a carpet, pictures and bigger, more comfortable seats, and I seem to remember that metal-panelled coaches were often painted to look like timber – these days a carriage that looked like it was made of timber would probably terrify passengers, who'd think that the carriage was likely to be unsafe. Sixty years ago timber probably suggested craftsmanship, skill and attention to detail.

I can still recall vividly the Southern Belle service from London. That seemed to be the epitome of superior rail travel – there were crystal lights, dining carriages with linen and silver service, and beautifully polished wood everywhere. The staff, I recall, were attentive to the nth degree. It was the sort of luxury you enjoyed on Concorde in more recent times.

■ PREVIOUS PAGE: HAULED BY A CLASS 5 4-6-0, A SPECIAL TRAIN FOR BLACKPOOL LEANS INTO THE CURVE AS IT APPROACHES STANDEDGE TUNNEL.

■ EDWARDIAN SPLENDOUR ON IARNRÓD ÉIREANN. C1955.

'First Class was comfortable
in the early part of the
century – especially the
dining cars'

Afternoon tea in the Salon-de-Luxe.
L. & N.W. American Special.

- Afternoon tea in the Salon-de-Luxe on a London & North Western Railway American boat train to Liverpool (above).
- Standards in Third Class were comparatively Spartan, as shown in this Midland Railway Third Class carriage (right), c.1920.

J.W. Robertson Scott remembered the sad days of decline:

In the 1940s and 1950s carriage interiors in my memory were uniformly drab and awful because there had been no money for decades to keep them up to scratch. Even First Class wasn't up to much, regardless of which region you found yourself travelling in. People think we travelled in coaches got up with cut glass and the finest polished mahogany but it's not true – the basic carriages may have dated back to the 1920s and in some areas even earlier, but they'd been repaired and refurbished and knocked about so often that nothing of any quality remained.

Certainly we looked back nostalgically to those gorgeous Edwardian carriages with top-quality upholstery, wide comfortable seats and a real sense that the colours of the interior were meant to match. First Class was comfortable in the early part of the century – particularly the dining cars, which I just about recall were all white linen, immaculately dressed waiters, sparkling electric lights and absurdly delicious food. I remember my father telling me about carriages got up like the Royal Carriage, with plush velvet seats and clerestory lights – a sort of raised central section in the carriage ceiling that ensured lots of natural light from above.

In the late 19th century Third Class tickets were known as penny-a-mile tickets after an Act of Parliament, which stated that train companies must run a few trains for working men and at a rate of a penny a mile. By this stage the Third Class carriages were enclosed (they'd been open to the elements like cattle trucks 40 years earlier).

J.W. Robertson Scott remembered those dim and distant days:
The early First Class carriages were made to represent three horse-drawn coach bodies joined together. At the end, outside, was a seat for the guard. Every railway had Second Class compartments. The earliest Second Class carriage, like the Third Class carriages, had no sides, the roof being supported by iron pillars. The passengers suffered horribly from wind and rain.

Eventually Third Class carriages were provided with seats and covered, but by the 1930s they were still very spartan and uncomfortable. For a long time on expresses, there were no Third Class carriages and I remember boys clambering over the wooden seats from one end of a carriage to the other.

Third Class carriage seats were often vandalized too – they were pencilled, often rudely, and also hacked by mischievous adults as well as idle lads. The thin cushions that eventually upholstered Third Class seats got cut and torn; electric-light bulbs were often smashed, so don't let anyone tell you that vandalism is entirely a modern phenomenon.

■ THE RELIEF DRIVER AND FIREMAN FOR THE 'FLYING SCOTSMAN' EXPRESS READ NEWSPAPERS WHILE RESTING IN ONE OF THE CARRIAGES, AUGUST 1928. THE GRESLEY 'A3' PACIFICS THAT HAULED THIS TRAIN HAD CORRIDOR TENDERS WHICH ALLOWED CREW CHANGEOVER WHILE THE TRAIN WAS ON THE MOVE.

PUTTING THEM IN THEIR PLACE
The Duke of Wellington was guest of honour at the opening of the Liverpool-Manchester line in 1830. Asked what he thought of the new railway trains he said he didn't approve of them 'because they encourage the lower orders to travel about.'

Third Class compartments had no window straps in the early days. First Class and Second Class passengers, in an age much given to hawking and spitting, were provided with spittoons. Thirds spat on the floor.

Anne Scott recalled First and Second Class travel in the late 1940s:

In First there was always carpet and the woodwork was beautifully cut and polished. The Great Western Railway and other companies commissioned beautiful paintings of the places they travelled to and reproductions of these were always to be found above the seats and each seat had a light above it. Best of all I remember the warm woollen seat upholstery – it was always renewed or repaired before it got tatty and, if memory serves, the carriages were always clean. That wasn't true I think of Second Class, which was far more basic – in fact it was really Third Class with a few improvements, because by the 1940s I seem to recall there was only First Class and Third, but then Third was rechristened Second and eventually became Standard, which is what it was under British Rail.

Ken Williams remembered how carriage designs changed over the years:

Well, anyone who has seen a preserved Edwardian or Victorian railway carriage will realize that those early carriages looked like Victorian and Edwardian sitting rooms – they were somehow all mahogany and chintz, with the dark colours people liked in those days.

Until the 1920s coach bodies were timber – oak or teak – and had timber panels. First the panelling became steel, then the frame, and those changes coincided with general increases in speed. It wasn't till after the war that the whole carriage structure became steel and most railways only had First and Third Class until the mid 1950s, when Third was simply renamed Second. Although corridor carriages came in during the early 20th century the old slam-door carriages where there were no corridors at all (or loos!) were still being built into the 1960s for shorter commuter journeys. Nothing of that world now remains.

Worries about women travelling by train were acute in the days before corridor trains appeared on the scene. A woman alone in a compartment could not reach any other compartment so there were rules about who could get in with a lone woman when the train stopped and what could be said. Parents of well-born girls were terrified and the train was seen as an invitation to scandal and immorality – which is why it wasn't until women

■ A RATHER LARGE HOLIDAYMAKER STRUGGLES TO GET PAST THE LUGGAGE IN A COACH CORRIDOR, 1950.

■ CHILDREN TRAVELLING ON A BRITISH RAILWAYS EXPRESS TRAIN SERVICE TO ST PANCRAS STATION, LONDON IN 1950.

began to work (middle class women, that is) during and after the Great War that train travel became less of a problem.

Sheila Kehoe remembered travelling just before World War II:

There was still a feeling that a woman travelling alone was somehow vulnerable but I think that is because we were brought up to see ourselves as weak and helpless – not being weak and helpless meant you were coarse and common. That absurd situation meant that all men were seen as either charming knights in shining armour and perfect gentlemen, or cads and rogues and sexually rapacious. The difficulty for women travelling on their own was that, whether any man you met was a sexual predator or the epitome of charm, you were at his mercy. It was simply assumed that women could not protect themselves and needed a chaperone or rules that would keep them safe.

My parents were very worried about me travelling alone so I hardly ever did it but even travelling with a friend – a female friend – you had certain unwritten rules to obey. If a man entered your carriage – or a woman – you always said good morning and you might very often exchange a few more

'THE LITTLE GOVERNESS'

'...the lady at the Governess Bureau had said: "You had better take an evening boat and then if you get into a compartment for 'Ladies Only' in the train you will be far safer than sleeping in a foreign hotel. Don't go out of the carriage; don't walk about the corridors and be sure to lock the lavatory door if you go there."'

Katherine Mansfield (1915)

RAILWAY ARCHITECTURE

CITADEL STATION, CARLISLE

■ BRITISH RAILWAYS CARRIAGE PRINT (ABOVE), PAINTED BY KENNETH STEEL IN THE 1950S, SHOWING CARLISLE CITADEL STATION.

■ COMPARTMENT ART SHOWED PLACES OF BEAUTY OR INTEREST NOW ACCESSIBLE TO RAIL TRAVELLERS, AS IN THIS BRITISH RAILWAYS CARRIAGE PRINT (RIGHT) OF HEMINGFORD GREY IN CAMBRIDGESHIRE, PAINTED BY L. SQUIRREL IN THE 1950S.

HEMINGFORD GREY, HUNTINGDONSHIRE

■ BEN LOYAL IN SUTHERLAND (BELOW) — A BRITISH RAILWAYS CARRIAGE PRINT PAINTED BY W. DOUGLAS MACLEOD IN 1950.

TRAVELLING EXHIBITIONS

Railway companies took great pride in the fixtures and fittings of their carriages and commissioned art from some of the best known artists of the day to adorn the space under the luggage rack. Subject matter usually related to the scenery and history of the region through which the train travelled.

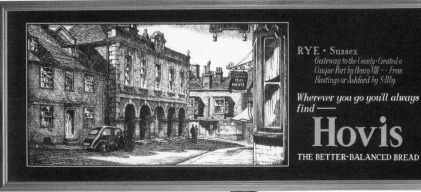

RYE · Sussex
Gateway to the County · Created a
Cinque Port by Henry VIII · · From
Hastings or Ashford by S·Rly.

Wherever you go you'll always
find ——

Hovis
THE BETTER-BALANCED BREAD

■ THE ATTRACTIVE TOWN OF RYE IN SUSSEX, IN AN UNIDENTIFIED ARTIST'S PRINT (ABOVE) FROM A SOUTHERN RAILWAY CARRIAGE, 1947.

■ THIS BRITISH RAILWAYS CARRIAGE PRINT FROM THE 1950S (BELOW), SHOWING ROBERT DUDLEY, EARL OF LEICESTER, HOLDING A KESTREL WHILE RIDING PAST KENILWORTH CASTLE, IS AN EXAMPLE OF THE RAILWAYS' PROMOTION OF HISTORICAL SITES AS TOURIST LOCATIONS.

ROBERT DUDLEY, EARL OF LEICESTER, AT KENILWORTH, THE HISTORIC CASTLE GRANTED TO HIM IN 1562 BY QUEEN ELIZABETH. THE RUINS OF MUCH OF THE CASTLE WHICH WAS FOUNDED IN THE 12TH CENTURY REMAIN TODAY.

FINE DINING

Before the British Rail sandwich established catering on the trains as a national laughing stock, standards were much higher. Railway companies took catering very seriously providing high quality silver service dining for its discerning customers.

■ BRITISH RAILWAYS CHEFS AT WORK IN A KITCHEN CAR, MARCH 1951.

■ A WAITER SERVING FIRST CLASS PASSENGERS ON THE 'HOOK CONTINENTAL' BOAT TRAIN, 20 JUNE 1961.

■ A BEAUTIFULLY LAID TABLE IN A LONDON & NORTH EASTERN RAILWAY DINING CAR, C.1930.

■ PASSENGERS IN LNER DINING CARS IN THE 1930S WERE OFFERED AN EXTENSIVE MENU OF FOOD, WHICH WAS COOKED FOR THEM ON THE TRAIN.

■ THE RAILWAY COMPANIES WERE PROUD OF THEIR RESTAURANT SERVICE, AS ADVERTISED IN 1928.

'The only sound would be the sound of one's train gathering speed'

A View From the Window

Until the 1920s most major cities were ringed by countryside that was little more than a half-day's ride by bicycle from the city centre. London's market gardens began at Barnes in the west, for example, and at Enfield in north London ancient farms could still be reached only along narrow, overgrown lanes.

Trunk roads, motorways and to a large extent the motor car itself were still things of some dimly imagined future. And compared to the car the railway unobtrusively took the passenger deep into this countryside and into the wilder regions of Wales, the South West and the northern uplands. Views from the window were one of the great pleasures of travel when trains went through this still apparently bucolic countryside.

The artist Denys Watkins Pitchford remembered travelling north from Enfield to his home in Northamptonshire in the 1920s:

I can't describe how pleasant railway travel was in those days. It was fast certainly, but not so fast that we hated to stop at small country stations along the way. I loved the forlorn look of these halts with a lonely signalbox here and there and the fields stretching away. The only sound would be the sound of one's train gathering speed and then the marvellous green of the countryside or the harsh black and white of winter landscapes. I never tired of it and I think that my brother and I looked forward to going home as much for the journey as for the getting there.

■ PASSENGERS ON THIS EX GWR 'HALL' CLASS 4-6-0 ENJOYED SPECTACULAR VIEWS ALONG THE DAWLISH SEA WALL IN DEVON (LEFT), C 1956.

■ CLASS '4575' 2-6-2T No.5517, THE CAMBRIAN COAST EXPRESS (BOTTOM LEFT) ENTERS THE PRETTY TOWN OF BARMOUTH, IN SNOWDONIA, IN JULY 1958.

■ A HUNSLET AUSTERITY SHUNTING LOCOMOTIVE (BELOW) ON THE CLIFF TOPS AT WHITEHAVEN IN CUMBRIA, IN THE EARLY 1970S.

Looking back from the 1920s, by which time he was an old man, John Neeve Masters recalled the steam travel of the Victorian era:

When the train came in puffing and smoking I saw just six railway coaches. They were all smoking carriages, and there were no notices up, not even about not spitting on the floor.

There were one or two who had never been in a railway train before and the astonishment on their faces was something to behold. The hedges and fields lay rich green in the summer heat and villages passed untroubled by the rushing impatient locomotive. It certainly was something to be remembered.

Well, father and I got to London Bridge Station all right. We stayed at an inn in Aldersgate Street and took a hansom cab to the Tower of London, the Bank, the Royal Exchange, and through Temple Bar. The last hansoms didn't disappear, astonishingly, until just before the Great War.

J.W. Robertson Scott remembered travelling by train through the grim suburbs of London and through pleasanter regions:

I'd chosen Oxfordshire because I wanted to be within an hour's journey by train of the capital – to see friends, visit the theatre and the library and so on, but no sooner had I got to London and finished whatever business I had on hand than I was desperate to get away again. In the countryside after a few weeks I missed the busyness and life of the city, and when I got on the train at Kingham or Charlbury and took my comfortable seat by the window with the warm sun coming through, I felt I was ready for an adventure. I rarely travelled to town in winter so my memories are of warm long days. As we sped

■ LOOKING BACK OVER BARMOUTH BRIDGE FROM THE DOWN CAMBRIAN COAST EXPRESS IN THE EARLY 1960S.

towards the city I was conscious of busier streets flashing by and more mess, but back in the 1930s you'd be surprised how much countryside there still was in areas where now there are only houses. Greenford and Perivale are now very unattractive suburbs, but in the 1930s I often saw a farmer plodding home on an old horse. They always sat sideways but you'd see them for an instant as the train crossed a bridge or neared a station. With Paddington only a few miles away blackness seemed to descend everywhere – sheer walls of brick, the backs of factories, wet and sooty; grimy little houses in endless rows; then the canal again. I can remember always being astonished when I saw a man fishing the canal – the Grand Union I suppose it would have been, somewhere near Kensal Rise. I simply couldn't believe that in all that grime and filth there could be anything bright and silver like a fish, but those fishermen can't have been sitting there for nothing.

As we approached Paddington itself the air would be quite indescribably smoky. If you went in winter you might easily walk out of the station into a pea-souper, a fog the like of which you cannot imagine if you haven't experienced it. They usually descended in winter, which is why I tended to stay in Oxford, but you knew before the train arrived if you were in trouble, because visibility

out of the window would be nil. Being teetotal and a lifelong non-smoker at a time when everyone seemed to smoke made it harder for me, with smoke in the carriages and smoke outside in the streets and squares.

But if I was going to the theatre or to work in the old round Reading Room at the British Museum my spirits would recover, because I felt that this was still the hub of the universe. London really was the pride of empire, and you sensed its might and were rather proud that you could come to it whenever you liked. By evening I'd be longing for the train. I never bought food on the platforms or on the train – somehow I never thought it was wholesome enough – but the view from the window growing ever cleaner and greener reconciled me to the prospect of two or three weeks or perhaps a month or more buried in one of the quietest villages in Oxfordshire.

■ STEAMING THROUGH CENTRAL WALES, BETWEEN SHREWSBURY AND SWANSEA

■ COMMUTERS CROSSING A BRIDGE BETWEEN PLATFORMS AT BIRMINGHAM NEW STREET STATION IN 1927.

■ AFTER THEIR DAY'S WORK, OUT-OF-TOWNERS BOARDING A SUBURBAN TRAIN AT WATERLOO STATION IN JANUARY 1972.

To Work and Back

It was the superb time-keeping of the old steam railways, not to mention the frequency of the service, that began the great British tradition of commuting to work.

When horses dominated the transport system commuting was unheard of, simply because it was an impossibility from a practical point of view. But with trains running at 60 and more miles an hour, even long journeys into town each day became perfectly feasible.

Julian Bell, who commuted from Henley into London every working day for more than 40 years, recalled a rather leisurely commuting atmosphere: *I regularly sat with the same people each day. Some got on before me and others appeared at stations closer to London. Of course occasionally we missed a familiar face but people tended to change jobs only rarely in those days, so the same faces generally cropped up year after year. I wouldn't say it was like seeing old friends every day, because even after a decade or more one never*

■ THE MORNING RUSH HOUR CROWD AT LIVERPOOL STREET STATION IN AUGUST 1928.

really made friends beyond perhaps the sort of friendly banter one might have with work colleagues.

To be honest we paid no attention to the paintings above the seats, the individual lights above our heads and all the other little details that we missed only once they were gone.

People complained about slam-door carriages without corridors but I rather liked them. I could smoke my pipe and no one dreamed of complaining – they were used to the smell of the steam and coal smoke drifting in the windows in summer, because of course in those days you could still open the windows. That wasn't always a good thing because children sometimes stuck their heads out and were killed, but there was something civilized about being able to open a window whenever you felt like it. These days when the air conditioning stops working there's no back-up system for opening the windows so in summer it can be dreadfully uncomfortable.

■ WAITING FOR A GREAT WESTERN RAILWAY WORKMEN'S TRAIN AT SLOUGH STATION, C.1907.

I don't remember playing cards or other games with my fellow passengers – people were friendlier up to a point in the steam days but there was no intimacy. The formalities of politeness were observed but we all knew they were just formalities. We said good morning and smiled and then settled to our newspapers. Everyone read The Times and The Daily Telegraph – women tended to read books or magazines, I recall. And there really were bowler hats and in the early 1950s I can just recall a few top hats worn still for the journey into the office!

'... there was something civilized about being able to open a window whenever you felt like it.'

THE RAILWAY NETWORK

The railway boom of the 19th and early 20th centuries really was that – new lines were built at an astonishing rate and into the most obscure corners of the country.

■ THIS ROUTE MAP OF THE BRITISH RAILWAYS
NETWORK WAS PRODUCED IN 1962 JUST PRIOR TO
THE SWINGEING BEECHING CUTS.

■ THE CAMBRIAN RAILWAYS
OWNED 230 ROUTE MILES IN
CENTRAL WALES UNTIL THEY
WERE ABSORBED BY THE GREAT
WESTERN RAILWAY IN 1922.

■ THIS TILE MAP OF THE LANCASHIRE &
YORKSHIRE RAILWAY CAN STILL BE SEEN AT
MANCHESTER VICTORIA STATION.

■ AN EARLY MAP SHOWING BRITAIN'S
RAILWAYS AND LINES OF NAVIGATION,
C.1845.

RAILWAY MAPS

Specialist railway maps showed the extraordinary development of the rail network and were a delight for those planning a journey.

■ THIS SOUTHERN RAILWAY ROUTE MAP OF 1935 ALSO SHOWS THE NUMEROUS FERRY CROSSINGS TO THE CONTINENT.

149. – LONDON. – Charing Cross Railway Station, South Eastern Railway

■ THE IMPOSING
FRONTAGE OF THE
SOUTH EASTERN
RAILWAY'S LONDON
TERMINUS AT CHARING
CROSS.

*'The railway was so exciting
and important that a purely
functional building was just
not acceptable.'*

Many stations were built in remote
out-of-the-way places on moors
and in the Highlands, but they
were also sited wherever the need
arose – high above ground level
sometimes (Charing Cross Station
in London is a good example) or
on bridges spanning the tracks
below. Ken Williams remembered
the occasional awkwardness caused
by the design of one station at
which he worked as a booking clerk
in the late 1930s:

*Southgate Station was built on a
bridge above the line and when you
saw the train coming you closed the
barrier for arrivals, but sometimes
I was a bit late closing it and I
caught a couple of people in the
midriff, which didn't go down well
at all!*

■ ALTHOUGH LESS IMPRESSIVE THAN THE GREAT CITY
TERMINI, MANY SMALL STATIONS HAD A DIGNITY
AND CHARM IN KEEPING WITH THEIR RURAL
SETTINGS.

■ SWANSEA VICTORIA STATION, THE TERMINUS FOR
TRAINS COMING FROM THE HEART OF WALES, WAS
CLOSED ON 13 JUNE 1964, AND IS NOW THE SITE
OF THE NATIONAL WATERFRONT MUSEUM. HERE, A
STANIER 'BLACK FIVE' 4-6-0 NO.45272 STANDS
AT THE PLATFORM HAVING COMPLETED ITS JOURNEY
FROM SHREWSBURY.

- A FINE ARRAY OF SEMAPHORES ON THE MAIN LINE NORTH FROM PRESTON ON THE WEST COAST MAIN LINE.
- THIS EARLY VICTORIAN PHOTOGRAPH OF YORK STATION CLEARLY SHOWS THE MAGNIFICENT, CURVING ROOF THAT STILL SURVIVES TODAY.
- ALTHOUGH THE HEREFORD TO GLOUCESTER RAILWAY WAS OPENED IN 1855 THE STATION AT BALLINGHAM DID NOT OPEN UNTIL 1908. THE LINE CLOSED IN 1964 AND BALLINGHAM STATION BUILDING IS NOW A PRIVATE RESIDENCE.

Tom Shackle, who was born in 1911, remembered his father, a station architect, who shared the Victorian belief in the importance of station architecture:

For those who designed and built the stations at the height of the railway's popularity, the need was to build to impress, which is why so many stations are designed in the Gothic style or like mediaeval castles, or Greek temples. The railway was so exciting and important that a purely functional building was just not acceptable. My father told me that no expense was spared in the materials used – costly stone and marble were used even in smaller provincial stations, stonemasons and woodcarvers were employed and the cost was seen as more than justified by the benefit – the main perceived benefit (perceived by the train company owners that is) was that travellers would be so impressed by the stations at which they began and ended their journeys that they would come back again and again.

Bridges and Tunnels

Bridges on the railway network were built in their tens of thousands to cope with roads, tracks, lanes, rivers, streams and even canals, but each one of them – from the smallest and simplest to enormously elaborate structures – was designed and built with the sort of care that made the early railway in Britain the envy of the world.

Ken Williams, an engineer on the Southern Railway for 40 years, recalled how vital the vast number of railway bridges were to the smooth running of the railway:

My first job was in Peterborough. Not the Peterborough you see today, with its ugly, endless ring roads and disastrously rebuilt city centre. When I knew it in the 1930s and 1940s it was a sleepy old market town. My first job in the railway engineers' drawing office was to draw all the railway bridges between Great Coates and Grimsby. The equipment and techniques used to make a technical drawing in those days would almost certainly have been familiar to Brunel and the engineers of the mid-Victorian era.

■ A 'JUBILEE' CLASS 4-6-0 HAULS A PASSENGER TRAIN OVER THE WELLAND (HARRINGWORTH) VIADUCT ON 14 MAY 1955. WHEN OPENED IN 1878 AS PART OF THE OAKHAM TO KETTERING LINE IT WAS THE LONGEST BRICK-BUILT VIADUCT IN BRITAIN.

'We drew on specially prepared linen, which seems incredibly old-fashioned now'

We drew on specially prepared linen, which seems incredibly old-fashioned now. Each piece of linen had a right side and a wrong side and obviously you had to draw on the right side, but before you started you treated the linen to a dusting of chalk. The chalk made the surface slightly rough, which helped it take the ink. But just avoiding smudging your lines took considerable skill – particularly when you remember that we used an ink pen that had to be filled from a bottle. I once asked why we had to draw so many bridges and was quickly told that without bridges there would be no railway – quite true too.

THE TAY BRIDGE DISASTER

The Tay Bridge Disaster of 28 December 1879 occurred when the central section of the newly opened Tay Bridge collapsed in a Force 10 gale, while a train was crossing it. The death toll was 75, the only survivor being the locomotive itself, which was lifted from the river bed, repaired and later returned to service. The tragedy is commemorated by the notorious Scottish rhymester William McGonagall in his poem 'The Tay Bridge Disaster'.

We used to say that you could always tell a draughtsman by the ticks of ink on the back of his hand – every time he was about to start on the linen he'd make a little mark on his wrist to make sure the ink was flowing.

Quite soon after I started we were sent out to get a feel for the surveyor's instruments. This was a way of teaching that harked back to the earliest days of the railway, but I found out how to use the level and the other instruments by watching others and then trying myself. Most of what we were doing concerned drawing the cracks on railway bridges, but the way the stones or the iron fitted together on those old bridges was a wonder.

I worked on bridges, embankments and earthworks and I remember how we still used old measurements such as chains. A chain is 22 yards.

As part of his final civil engineer's exam, Ken had to draw a railway bridge. It didn't matter which one but it had to be perfect. Once he'd done that, and assuming everything else went well, he would become a member of the Institution of Civil Engineers.

■ ON THE LAST DAY OF SERVICE ON THE HAYLING ISLAND
BRANCHLINE (LEFT), CLASS A1X 0-6-0T No.32662
TRUNDLES OVER LANGSTONE BRIDGE WITH A TRAIN
FROM HAVANT.

*I drew a railway bridge near the sea. I calculated all the sections
of steel required and produced my drawing. I was really proud
of it as it included every last rivet, angle and flange. I had to
get it signed by the bridge engineer, but when he saw it he asked
me where it was. Well, it was actually close to the Essex coast.
When he heard that, he made me add a quarter of an inch to all
the angles because of the corrosion caused by saltwater breezes.
I remember being impressed by that level of thinking. Anyway,
with that drawing I'd finally passed the exams and for years
afterwards whenever I went with my family on the line that
crossed the bridge I used to point it out to them. I was really
proud of it but they used to say: 'What? Is that it?' I think they
were expecting something like the Forth Bridge!*

■ CLOSED RAILWAYS
ENGENDER A
NOSTALGIC
ATMOSPHERE (ABOVE)
AND NEVER MORE
SO THAN AT THE
MAGNIFICENT VIADUCT
AT SHANKEND ON
THE FORMER NORTH
BRITISH RAILWAY'S
'WAVERLEY ROUTE'
BETWEEN CARLISLE
AND EDINBURGH.

■ A LONDON TO
BRIGHTON ELECTRIC
TRAIN (ABOVE)
CROSSES THE OUSE
VALLEY VIADUCT IN
JANUARY 1985.

■ THE FAMOUS SONNING
CUTTING (RIGHT) ON
THE FORMER GREAT
WESTERN RAILWAY'S
MAIN LINE BETWEEN
READING AND
TWYFORD. EXCAVATED
COMPLETELY BY
MANPOWER, THE LINE
WAS OPENED IN 1840.

'They ran screaming from the tunnel, convinced that they had broken through to the devil's own kingdom'

- ON THE ISLE OF WIGHT RAILWAY (ABOVE), CLASS '02' 0-4-4T No.27 'MERSTONE' PULLS OUT OF THE TUNNEL BEFORE ARRIVING AT VENTNOR STATION.

- DURING THE LAST FEW YEARS OF STEAM ON BRITISH RAILWAYS (LEFT), STANIER 8F 2-8-0 No.48053 APPROACHES DOVES HOLE TUNNEL IN THE PEAK DISTRICT WITH A DOWN FREIGHT IN JULY 1965.

'THE SIGNALMAN'

'... His post was in as solitary and dismal a place as ever I saw. On either side, a dripping-wet wall of jagged stone, excluding all view but a strip of sky; the perspective one way only a crooked prolongation of this great dungeon; the shorter perspective in the other direction terminating in a gloomy red light, and the gloomier entrance to a black tunnel, in whose massive architecture there was a barbarous, depressing, and forbidding air.'

from 'The Signalman', Charles Dickens

As the men dug and hacked ever deeper in the appallingly hot, badly lit and entirely unventilated system, they noticed that the ground beneath them was beginning to move. The men stood back quickly, focusing their dim lights on the place. Minutes later the tunnel floor gave way and the navvies were horrified to see below them shadowy figures and dim lights moving. They ran screaming from the tunnel, convinced that they had broken through to the devil's own kingdom.

In fact Stephenson and the other engineers involved in digging the tunnel had no idea that another tunnel was being dug in the same area – tunnel depth and trajectory calculations were then in their infancy, so bumping into unexpected things was quite common. But in this instance it took several hours to convince the men that they were not in fact about to be carried off by Old Nick. The other tunnel was being dug by Joseph Williamson, an extremely wealthy retired tobacco merchant who built miles of tunnels and caverns under the Edge Hill district of Liverpool in order to provide jobs for unemployed men.

In Scotland at least one disused railway tunnel was used to grow commercial quantities of mushrooms and during the war tunnels were found to be so solid and well made that a number were used as security depots and even offices.

Driver Reg Coote remembered that the shedmaster at Orpington in Kent moved his office into a disused tunnel for the duration of the war!

■ Standard Bagnall 0-6-0ST 'Enterprise' (above) on shunting duties at the Preston Dock Authority in the mid 1960s.

■ Built in 1889, ex-North British Railway Class Y9 0-4-0 saddle tank No.68102 (left) was ideal for short trip working around the sharply curved dock lines of Scotland. This example is permanently attached to a wooden tender.

DOCKS AND HARBOURS

The movement of goods was revolutionized by the arrival of the railways at docks and harbours – speed and efficiency were transformed as the old horse-and-cart system faded into history and rails were laid right to the shipside.

■ ONE OF THE LAST HAVENS OF STEAM POWER IN BRITAIN WAS IN DOCKLAND AND WHITEHAVEN BECAME A NOTED LOCATION. HERE 'VICTORIA', AN 0-4-0 SADDLE TANK BUILT BY PECKETT OF BRISTOL IN 1942, TAKES A BREATHER BETWEEN SPELLS OF HAULING WAGONS UP TO THE BOATS FROM THE SURROUNDING COLLIERIES. IN COMMON WITH MOST BRISTOL-BUILT INDUSTRIAL ENGINES, 'VICTORIA' HAD OUTSIDE CYLINDERS AND HER SHORT WHEELBASE ENABLED HER TO NEGOTIATE THE TIGHT CURVES ALONG THE QUAYSIDE.

■ AT RYDE PIER HEAD (RIGHT) IN AUGUST 1964 AN EX-LONDON & SOUTH WESTERN 'O2' CLASS 0-4-4T WAITS TO DEPART WITH A BOAT TRAIN, AS A PADDLE STEAMER DISEMBARKS ITS PASSENGERS IN THE BACKGROUND.

■ EX-SR 'USA' CLASS 0-6-0T NO.30064 SHUNTING NEAR THE OCEAN TERMINAL AT SOUTHAMPTON IN MAY 1967.

85

On the Mainline

The long process of working your way up from cleaner to passed cleaner and then driver wasn't the end of the story. Once you were driving, there were different links and the top link gave the chance to drive passenger trains and expresses. As an express driver you were a member of an élite club.

Bill Sidwell, a railway engineer for more than 40 years, started work in 1927. He remembered that despite their status the express drivers weren't financially better off:

If an express driver pulled up alongside a shunting engine at Euston and the driver shouted over to the shunting engine driver, 'What price your little loco?' the little loco driver would always shout back, 'Same as yours – 90 bob a week!'

Of course the level of responsibility on the expresses was high as passengers were involved, and with each passing decade speeds increased dramatically. Back in the final decade of the 19th century things had been very different on express trains, as J.W. Robertson Scott recalled:

On our local Maryport and Carlisle Railway, Mr Carrick, who had been looking into the matter, reported speeds as: express goods 40 miles an hour, passenger expresses 30, locals 25, ordinary goods 20, and, on a branch, 15.

■ EX-GWR 'KING' CLASS 4-6-0 No. 6015 'KING RICHARD III' WAITS TO DEPART FROM BRISTOL TEMPLE MEADS WITH AN EXPRESS FOR PADDINGTON ON 3 SEPTEMBER 1960.

'The level of responsibility on the express was high'

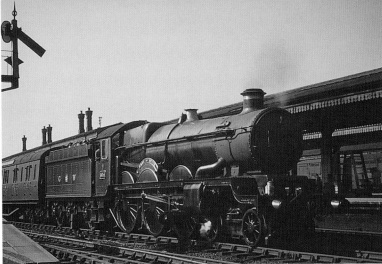

■ DESIGNED BY CHARLES COLLETT AS A DEVELOPMENT OF THE 'STAR' CLASS LOCOS, THE GREAT WESTERN RAILWAY 'CASTLE' CLASS 4-6-0 LOCOMOTIVES (ABOVE) WERE AMONG THE MOST SUCCESSFUL OF THEIR KIND IN THE WORLD.

■ ONLY SIX MONTHS BEFORE THE END OF STEAM ON BRITISH RAILWAYS, STANIER CLASS 5 4-6-0 NO.44690 (RIGHT) WAITS AT PRESTON STATION WITH A BLACKPOOL NORTH TO MANCHESTER PARCELS TRAIN ON 10 FEBRUARY 1968.

By 1910 things had moved on, but competition among passenger express drivers was fierce, as George P. Neale remembered:

All the drivers doing the same class of work, working for instance the broad-gauge expresses between London and Swindon, were formed into one corps technically known as a link. Every pound of coal and every pint of oil that goes into each man's engine was debited to him and at the end of the week the total was made up and divided by the number of miles his engine has run. The men were then arranged in order of merit, that is, of economy of fuel and oil consumption.

■ A VERY BEDRAGGLED 'CASTLE' CLASS 4-6-0, NO.7024 'POWIS CASTLE', HEADS OUT OF GLOUCESTER WITH THE 8.00 (SATURDAYS ONLY) WOLVERHAMPTON (LOW LEVEL) TO ILFRACOMBE TRAIN ON 22 AUGUST 1964.

■ Rebuilt 'West Country' 4-6-2 No.34032 'Camelford' and unrebuilt 'Battle of Britain' Class 4-6-2 No.34064 'Fighter Command' wait at Waterloo with trains for Weymouth on 24 June 1964.

■ Ex-LNER Class 'A3' 4-6-2 No.60074 'Harvester' departs from Leeds with the northbound 'Queen of Scots' express.

Of course for a single week, extra load, greasy rails or whatever might affect a man's position, but in the long run the man who comes out top is the best driver – he can do his work to time with the most scientific economy of force. A driver felt the loss of a good position on the coal sheet much as a boy feels on being sent to the bottom of his form at school.

Harry Ross, a fireman and latterly signalman who started work at Chester in 1935 as a junior porter, remembered how coal was allocated between various trains:

As a general rule freight trains didn't get good coal – that was kept for the passenger trains, especially the expresses to King's Cross.

Harry also remembered key differences between the treatments of trains in different areas:

The man in the box – the signalman – always knew exactly what times the trains were running to and how many wagons were on each train. He'd had to know that to know if they would fit in a loop. But it was all different on the Great Western – there the signalman was always asking where the expresses were. He often hadn't a clue!

Jim McClelland worked the *Mallard* – a record-breaking train – from Newcastle to Carlisle ('She was truly extraordinary,' he says) but the real record breaker was the LNER A4. With its streamlined shape it was designed for speed – and in fact an A4 still holds the world speed record for a steam locomotive, at 126 mph.

But records were nothing without style, and the style of an earlier age was recalled by porter and guard John Kerley:

Old Gore, the stationmaster at King's Cross, wore a top hat and tails every day and always saw important express trains such as the Flying Scotsman *off in person at 10am on Fridays.*

Richard Hardy, who started work in 1941 and eventually reached the British Railways Board, remembered the *Flying Scotsman* and the skill of its driver:

I rode on the famous 4472 Flying Scotsman *driven by Bob Foster. It was an education to see Bob making small delicate alterations to the valve travel to suit the road – level, uphill or down.*

Another fine driver, Alf Cartwright, stopped an express by mistake at a station and was given a roasting by the stationmaster. Calm as you like he replied: 'We'd better go then. It's a long time since we saw you, so we stopped to see how you were going on.'

■ 'JUBILEE' CLASS
4-6-0 NO.45708
'RESOLUTION'
CLIMBS TO MARSDEN
WITH A SATURDAY
SCARBOROUGH TO
MANCHESTER TRAIN.

FEATS OF ENGINEERING

The days of steam travel may be long gone, but the impressive feats of architecture created for the railways, the mighty bridges and breath-taking viaducts, have transformed the landscape of Britain for ever.

■ THE BROAD SWEEP OF THE KNUCKLAS VIADUCT (RIGHT) GAVE PASSENGERS ON THE TRAINS BETWEEN SHREWSBURY AND SWANSEA BREATHTAKING VIEWS OF THE WELSH COUNTRYSIDE.

■ AROUND 300 MEN WERE EMPLOYED IN THE BUILDING OF THE BROADSANDS VIADUCT (BELOW RIGHT), ON THE PAIGNTON TO DARTMOUTH LINE. MASONRY WAS USED INSTEAD OF TIMBER, AND THE CONSTRUCTION TOOK FROM AUTUMN 1859 TO SPRING 1861.

■ ISAMBARD KINGDOM BRUNEL'S ROYAL ALBERT BRIDGE AT SALTASH WAS OPENED IN 1859 AND IS STILL IN SERVICE. ITS GRACEFUL DESIGN AND ENGINEERING BRILLIANCE REMAINS UNEQUALLED.

■ ELEGANT IRONWORK DISPLAYED AT THE LONDON & SOUTH WESTERN RAILWAY'S VIADUCT AT MELDON IN DEVON (RIGHT).

- STANIER 'BLACK FIVE' (ABOVE) CROSSES INVERSHIN VIADUCT WITH A COMBINED RCTS/SLS SPECIAL IN JUNE 1962. THE TWO LEADING COACHES ARE PRESERVED CALEDONIAN RAILWAY STOCK.

- THE SWING SECTION OF THE SEVERN RAILWAY BRIDGE (RIGHT), HERE SEEN IN 1965, ALLOWED BOATS TO TRAVEL ALONG THE GLOUCESTER & SHARPNESS CANAL. THE BRIDGE WAS SERIOUSLY DAMAGED BY AN OIL BARGE IN 1960 AND WAS SUBSEQUENTLY DISMANTLED.

- THE CONNEL BRIDGE (LEFT) CARRIED BOTH ROAD AND RAIL ACROSS LOCH ETIVE UNTIL THE CLOSURE OF THE BALLACHULISH BRANCHLINE ON 28 MARCH 1966.

The Freight Carriers

Bulk carriage of goods began in earnest with the canals of the 18th century, and bulk carriage combined with bulk manufacture lowered prices and made goods available to the poor that were once unimaginable luxuries. This process accelerated with the railway boom as goods were moved quickly and even more efficiently – and in vast bulk – around the country.

The vital importance of freight in the steam era was recalled by shedmaster Richard Hardy:

It took me a total of eight years to become a shedmaster. I was finally given my own shed at Woodford on the Great Central, where I managed nearly 300 men and more than 50 engines – a tall order for a young man – but it was a job I loved and it made me realize that at the heart of the railway, in a sense, was freight.

At Woodford, our enginemen worked to Marylebone, Nottingham, Banbury and Sheffield with passenger trains but our shed was largely freight – to Banbury, Neasden, and the night express freight trains from Marylebone to Sheffield and Manchester.

Freight work was considerable in those days because there were no motorways and the massive container lorries of the modern world simply didn't exist. If you had freight to move you had to use the railways, which meant that we laboured under great responsibility. The system of records and accounts that allowed the nationwide movement of freight with only rare mishaps was impressive in its sophistication, if laborious by the standards of today. Everything was checked on to the train and off again – frequently several times!

Engineer Bill Sidwell remembered the enthusiasm of railway staff, either dealing with important trains or humble freight:

They were a great bunch and whether a problem arose with a Royal train or a humble freight wagon someone could always be found to sort the situation out. But of course as in all walks of life the railways were subject to human error. Freight trains were probably more prone to problems because with the best will in the world the locomotives used for freight were considered workhorses – they didn't need to be sleek and impressive-looking like passenger locomotives.

Most accidents I can recall – and there were regular freight derailments – were due to human error. The worst I remember happened on Sharnbrook Viaduct near Bedford. The signalman let a 100-wagon coal train through and it ran into another coal train. The loco and tender and 30 wagons swept over the side of the viaduct and the driver and fireman were killed. It was a terrible mess, but when you think that the whole system in the steam days was run using only men and mechanical aids it is a tribute to their skill that so few accidents – freight or passenger – actually did occur.

■ A DAILY TRAIN LEAVING W & A GILBEY THE WINEMERCHANTS' EXPORT WAREHOUSE WITH GOODS FOR THE DOCKS.

■ A STANIER CLASS '8F' 2-8-0 WITH A SOUTHBOUND FREIGHT TRAIN AT SUGAR LOAF SUMMIT ON THE CENTRAL WALES LINE, MAY 1964.

Surrey-based fireman Ray Beeson recalled the special techniques used for freight:

The process of bringing the train to a halt was also a big part of the fireman's job – with loose-coupled freight wagons (ie wagons with no brakes of their own) I would start braking using the turned handbrake on the tender. That would bring the wagons together, so you'd have captured the whole weight of the train ready for the driver to put the engine brake on.

One or two bits of our area were notorious – Virginia Water Bank, between Reading and Feltham, was an absolute bugger and there was a very steep section between Reading and Redhill known as Dorking Bank. It was places like those two that made it absolutely essential that you knew the road and your engine and your load, particularly if it was freight – if you didn't know your stuff you would almost certainly get stuck on that Reading-Redhill section, with all the timetable consequences that would entail.

There were different skills, too, with passenger as opposed to freight working – with freight you had to start braking a lot earlier because of all those loose-coupled wagons with no brakes. Passenger trains all had continuous brakes on all carriages.

In parts of East Anglia freight trains carried vast amounts of agricultural produce in the summer and autumn and in Scotland special trains were laid on at the ports, as Sandy Begg recalled:

At Kittybrewster I worked on trains that covered the area to Elgin, Peterhead and Ballater. It was mostly freight work and from the ports at Peterhead and Fraserburgh tons of fish to be moved. The fishing season lasted just six weeks, but the extra work these created was incredible – they were the busiest six weeks of the year for the railway workers.

■ A London & North Western Railway 10-ton coal wagon.

■ A BR Standard Class 4MT 4-6-0 climbs towards Ribblehead Viaduct on the Settle & Carlisle line with a northbound freight in the 1960s.

'... with freight you had to start braking a lot earlier'

Sandy Begg also remembered freight work in Edinburgh and Leith:

Here even in the 1950s a lot of the work of moving goods around the dockyard was still done by horses and the steam engines were rather primitive, with only hand brakes rather than steam brakes.

I knew horses were important at Leith when early on in my time there one of the drivers shouted 'Whoa!' at me!

LNER still had about 500 cart-horses at work in Edinburgh. They pulled unusual three-wheeled wagons that had been specifically designed to turn in restricted spaces. Lots of the lads on the engines had worked with these horses. I can remember every team of horses had a tracer boy – a boy who sat on one of the horses to help encourage them up steep inclines.

■ A STANIER CLASS '8F' PASSES THE NEAT SIGNAL BOX AT SUGAR LOAF SUMMIT ON THE CENTRAL WALES LINE IN MAY 1964. THE SIGNALMAN WILL EXCHANGE THE SINGLE LINE TOKEN IF HIS TROUSERS DON'T FALL DOWN!

■ OOPS! EX-LMS '3F' JINTY 0-6-0T, NO.47649 HAS GOT ITSELF INTO TROUBLE WHILE SHUNTING A VENTILATED FRUIT VAN AT STAFFORD.

Branchline and Suburban

Away from the famous expresses that hurtled between major cities, plain workhorse engines kept the vital network of branchlines and suburban services going right across the country.

Sheila Kehoe remembered visiting friends in Hertfordshire and Essex before the war:

By today's standards the little trains we took were probably slow, but we loved the gentle rattle across the countryside and because we didn't travel too quickly you could read the names of the stations, so it was a pleasure. I really do think that people in those days didn't get all het up at the relative slowness of travel. The pace of life was slower and that was accepted because people didn't expect to travel 50, 80 or 100 miles to work each day and then back in the evening. No wonder they panic about faster and faster trains now when so much of their lives is spent on them. In my day almost everyone worked locally and took local trains to do it. Far fewer women worked and so you would see them on local trains visiting relatives or meeting each other somewhere for lunch or tea. I don't think I'm looking back with rose-tinted specs – well, perhaps a bit!

■ ON 29 JUNE 1963 THE LMS 4MT IVATT 'MOGUL' 2-6-0 NO. 43011 (BELOW LEFT) STOPS AT THE PICTURESQUE STATION OF LANGHOLM IN DUMFRIESSHIRE.

Vinsun Gulliver remembered local lines decades before Beeching:

I passed fit for driving on Shrove Tuesday – I can't remember which year but I remember it was Shrove Tuesday and well before 1930. The most exciting thing about it all of course was that it meant I earned a bit more money. I drove the branchline and suburban trains, but I drove them all over the place to Glossop, Stalybridge, Macclesfield, Liverpool, all local stuff; but many of the lines I worked disappeared with the Beeching Cuts. In those days of course we weren't romantic about steam; it was hard work, much harder than diesel or electric and they were made – those little workhorse engines I mean – simply to do a job. They weren't fancy or smart or particularly powerful like the famous engines but they quietly got on with the job – like the people who drove them!

■ GRAIN HALT, C.1910, WAS A SIMPLE WOODEN STRUCTURE ON THE BRANCHLINE TO PORT VICTORIA ON THE ISLE OF GRAIN IN KENT.

'... because we didn't travel too quickly you could read the names of the stations, so it was a pleasure.'

■ As the high tide laps dangerously close, Ex-LB&SCR Class 'A1X' 0-6-0T No.32650 departs from North Hayling with a train for Havant on the last day of service, 2 November 1963.

■ Introduced in 1883, Drummond Caledonian Railway's 'standard goods' Class 2F' 0-6-0 No.57441 is still at work in May 1959 at Kirriemuir Station with a local freight. The coal merchant has filled his cart and is persuading his horse to tackle the steep climb up to the village.

Bill Sidwell remembered driving a suburban train near Manchester:
We'd just pulled into the station and we were watching the passengers leave when a little old lady noticed the name of the loco – she was called **Girl Guide** *– and smiled up at us. 'How nice,' she said. 'I used to be a Girl Guide.' I remember the old driver mumbled after she'd left, 'God help any Girl Guide who's as rough as this old girl!' What he meant was that the loco was a good one but bloody uncomfortable to ride.*

The intricacy of the old branchline network can be judged by Bill's memory of routes to Blackpool:
From Mirfield there are 27 variations of the route to Blackpool (if you can believe it); each driver had to know the particular route he was going to take. It was a bit of a nightmare but we got there in the end.

Safety on branchlines was just as important as elsewhere, as Harry Ross remembered:
Single-line working on branchlines gave me some of the most interesting experiences because occasionally I had to act as a pilotman. On one occasion I was in charge of single-line working between Staverton and Charwelton. I had to put the system into operation on the first available train, which happened to be a

'Safety on branchlines was just as important as elsewhere'

- IN A SCENE REMINISCENT OF A 'PICTURE POST' IMAGE, A SOUTH EASTERN & CHATHAM RAILWAY 'H' CLASS 0-4-4T CROSSES THE MAIN ROAD AT CANTERBURY.

- 30 DECEMBER 1966 WAS THE PENULTIMATE DAY OF STEAM ON THE ISLE OF WIGHT. HERE, CLASS 'O2' 0-4-4T NO.16 'VENTNOR' PAUSES AT BRADING WITH THE 12.30 RYDE TO SHANKLIN TRAIN.

passenger train called the **Farnborough Flyer**. *I was at Staverton Road waiting for this train and when it arrived I had to ride on the footplate of the leading loco. I should add that this train was double-headed – in other words, pulled by two locos. Anyway, I got up on the footplate and there was my old friend George Tasker. He was delighted to see me but in a foul mood because I was causing his train to be delayed.*

To put single-line working into operation I'd had to issue the signalman with special forms, which had to be countersigned by me. I also had to show myself to all the staff working on the track, for no movement could take place without my being there to see it. All these precautions show just how careful we were about safety.

Swindon-based driver Fred Simpson recalled that if they were stopped at a country signal miles from anywhere the footplatemen would curse their luck, but occasionally things were not quite as bad:

We used to get stopped for ages every now and then at a signal near which an aunt of mine lived. More than once we dashed off to her house for a fry up. And at another signal there was a nearby pub – I think the men used to pray that if they were going to be held up it would be at that signal! Mind you I did hear that, what with the war being on, as often as not they got to the pub only to find they'd run out of beer!

Fred spent his first three years as a passed cleaner, firing on pannier tanks – 'They were really good little side-tank engines,' he recalled – but the lack of maintenance made even these little workhorses difficult.

They were used for shunting and for local passenger work and one or two survived the wholesale destruction of steam engines in the 1960s. For many years, as Fred explains, one helped keep London Underground going:

For decades they kept it for shunting when the electricity failed, but I suspect it's long gone now.

At Chester most of the engines were small. Fireman Harry Ross recalled:

We had C13 tanks, 442s, N5s, but not the superheated ones, J10s and the Sentinel Railcar, a passenger car with the engine at one end. It did local trips from Chester to Northgate.

■ INTRODUCED IN 1916, PICKERSGILL CALEDONIAN RAILWAY 3P 4-4-0 No.54465 STANDS AT THE NEAT TERMINUS STATION AT BLAIRGOWRIE.

THE RAILWAY COMPANIES

The absorption of more than a hundred private railway companies into four major operators eased the complexities of the growing rail network but did not bring uniformity – each of the big four companies had its own character and reputation.

Before the Big Four

The railway began with private enterprise and dozens of companies but the lure of rationalization and standardization led first to the birth of the big four companies and eventually to British Rail.

However, in the view of some a multitude of companies wasn't all bad. Ken Williams remembered:
I think people exaggerate the difficulties of having lots of operators – there were difficulties certainly, but it wasn't really in the interests of the various companies to make life too difficult for passengers even though they knew they had a captive market, unlike today when people can get in their cars if they get fed up. The fact that Bradshaw, *the famous railway timetable book, was published and sold for so long, well over a century, shows you that travel across country and over several different operators was complicated; but it has always been complicated, simply because changing trains and catching connecting trains will occasionally lead to trouble – and it can seem irritating, just because everyone would prefer a straight run through and no changing. But how could that be organized if you wanted to go from Whitstable in Kent to Christchurch in Dorset, or Skegness to Carlisle? My father regularly crossed the main routes in the old days and he said that part of the fun was working it all out. He lived from the time there were 123 railway companies into the era of the big four, and didn't think that was much better!*

Tom Shackle took a slightly different view:
The existence of the big four companies certainly reduced the complexities and the cost of travel, although the four regions competed with each other and drivers and other workers in one region always thought their rivals in the other regions were rubbish! But this sort of thing happened within the same region too – drivers didn't mix socially with guards, signalmen didn't mix with management and so on. In the very

■ PREVIOUS PAGE: A WORKMAN PAINTS THE GREAT WESTERN RAILWAY'S NEW MONOGRAM AT PADDINGTON STATION, LONDON, AUGUST 1934.

■ OPENING DAY AT LAMBOURNE STATION ON THE LAMBOURNE VALLEY RAILWAY IN BERKSHIRE, 4 APRIL 1898.

■ THIS 'TENNENT' CLASS 2-4-0 NO.1464 WAS IN USE ON THE NORTH EASTERN RAILWAY, c1890.

early days it was just the same, although the early companies were often very small – like the London and Croydon Railway, for example.

The truth is that each region wanted to be the best, but they knew they had to hand passengers over gently between companies and they tried to do it as well as they could despite bureaucracy. Before the British Rail era the lack of marketing men meant that ticketing was simpler anyway, as tickets and pricing weren't geared as they are now to getting people off the rush hour trains and on to the less busy services. The science of sales and pricing strategies was then unknown.

Denys Watkins Pitchford thought travel in the early part of the 20th century had a charm that actually was linked to the number of train operators: *Well, getting across a difficult route where you had to go between train companies wasn't as difficult you might think in the early days, although I can only really remember my father talking about it, as I was 18 when the big four were created in 1923.*

The point is that no one was able to compare train travel with anything better – very few people had cars and the ones they had weren't reliable or fast, and there were no motorways. Going to Devon from London by car was an arduous day's journey, for example – a journey you could do in the train far quicker even allowing for slow trains, signals, country stations and so on. The train was the best form of travel there was, particularly if you got the fast train. As there were no alternatives that were cheaper or better people were more forgiving, and they looked quite calmly at the prospect of fearsomely

> '... *the train was the best form of travel there was, particularly if you got the fast train*'.

■ A MIDLAND RAILWAY 4-2-2 WAITS TO DEPART FROM GLOUCESTER EASTGATE WITH AN EXPRESS TO THE NORTH IN THE EARLY 20TH CENTURY.

■ DESIGNED BY T. W. WORDSELL, THE NORTH EASTERN RAILWAY 'B. T. P'. CLASS 0-4-4 WELL TANK NO.91 WAS BUILT IN FEBRUARY 1885 AT GATESHEAD.

complicated journeys with all sorts of perilous connections and changes of train and jumps between train companies that, by the standards of the big four companies, were very small indeed. I think it gave men like my father the chance to take control and work out something apparently complicated that impressed their womenfolk. My mother was always astonished at my father's abilities to organize train travel. She would organize the coachman to take us to the station – hardly difficult as it was our coach and our coachman – and then my father would take over with a magisterial air for the really challenging bit; but he loved it.

■ LNER 4-4-0 TANK LOCOMOTIVE NO.7 HEADS TOWARDS HIGH BARNET WITH A COMMUTER TRAIN FROM KING'S CROSS IN THE 1890S.

■ A LONDON & SOUTH WESTERN RAILWAY ADAMS OUTSIDE CYLINDER 4-4-0 BUILT BY THE LEGENDARY GORTON FOUNDRY OF BEYER PEACOCK IN 1890.

The Big Four: LNER

Each of the big four railway companies had its own traditions, character and perhaps most significantly, reputation.

Richard Hardy thought about a career with the LMS (London, Midland and Scottish Railway) but as a former public schoolboy – he was educated at Marlborough – he opted for the LNER (London and North Eastern Railway). He recalled why:

I went straight into a job as an apprentice at Doncaster. I can remember the exact date – it was January 17, 1941. An older friend at school had gone to the LMS and I thought, vaguely, I ought to follow him, but my heart was in the LNER, and when I saw Col Pullein-Thompson, the careers advisor, and asked his advice, he went straight to the point: 'Go on the LNER boy! Gentlemen at the top!'

■ LNER Ivatt 4-4-2 No. 3283 (below) storms up the East Coast main line with an express in the 1930s.

'Go to LNER boy! Gentlemen at the top!'

THE FIRST OF THEIR KIND
In 1935 the first major class of streamlined locomotives to be used in Britain were deployed on the King's Cross to Newcastle route. These Gresley Class 'A4' Pacifics were considered a real propaganda coup for the LNER. In 1938 the No. 4468 Mallard – another 'A4' class locomotive – achieved a record speed of 126mph on a test run down Stoke Bank.

Driver Dick Potts recalled the awe in which LNER locomotives were held:

They were simply the best – or at least I thought so. I used to go train spotting at Hitchin whenever I had any free time. This would have been 1947 or early 1948. I loved it because coming from Birmingham I'd never seen LNER engines before and here they all were – Pacifics, A4s, all thundering in and out of the station. It was heaven. I used to sit watching them for hours, even in the dark. In fact in the dark it was particularly exciting, because a lot of those drivers used to thrash their engines and you'd see sparks from the wheels and streams of fire from the chimneys.

■ LNER GRESLEY 'A4'
CLASS PACIFIC 4-6-
2,'EMPIRE OF INDIA',
THEN NUMBERED 11,
STANDS WITH A TRAIN
AT NEWCASTLE ON 11
AUGUST 1947.

■ A TRAIN OF VINTAGE
WOODEN CARRIAGES
PULLED BY LNER 'E4'
CLASS 2-4-0 No.7490
AT CAMBRIDGE IN
JUNE 1938.

Dick also recalled those occasions when a driver from one area, in this case his father, had to deal with engines from another area:

I remember my dad got landed with a Southern engine once and he hadn't a clue what to do with it. And remember, in those days you couldn't go and ask for a few lessons – there weren't any lessons to be had. In my dad's case he just got by as best he could working by trial and error and relying on the fact that some things were standard – all engines would have a regulator of course – but you never really understood an engine unless you drove it regularly.

Harry Ross recalled a key practical difference between LNER and the other regions:

On the footplate of LNER locomotives the controls and various features would be in different places on different engines. By contrast Great Western locomotives had footplates that were standard – everything was always in the same place and of a standard design. Take the fire-hole door. On the Great Western the fire-hole door was oval-shaped, on Great Central engines it might be oval-shaped or square, as it was on North Eastern engines. There were many other differences of course too – Southern Railway always seemed the quiet one to us, GWR was too full of itself; LNER was all about locos and speed records!

■ IN THE BLEAK MID-WINTER LNER 'A3' CLASS 4-6-2 NO.2545, 'DIAMOND JUBILEE' (ABOVE LEFT), AT THE HEAD OF A TRAIN AT RED HALL IN JANUARY 1939.

■ EX-NER ROBINSON 4-6-0 NO.928 HEADS UP AN EXTRAORDINARY MIXED TRAIN ON THE LNER IN THE LATE 1920S.

■ LNER GRESLEY 'A3' PACIFIC No.4472, 'GAY CRUSADER' AWAITS DEPARTURE
FROM KING'S CROSS WITH A TRAIN FOR THE NORTH IN THE 1930S.

■ RESPLENDENT IN A NEW COAT OF PAINT, LNER 'C1' CLASS 4-4-2 No.3286
POSES AT HITCHIN IN JUNE 1937.

Ken Williams always felt that the LNER fancied
itself a cut above the rest:

*It was one of those things you heard a lot of
railwaymen say – on the Southern they'd say
the LNER boys were a bit stuck up or too full of
themselves, but I think some of the bad feeling
was just banter and they didn't really mean it,
although the lads on the Southern sometimes
felt a bit suburban compared to the men on the
LNER – hardly surprising, given that London to
Brighton could not really be compared with those
long journeys from London to York, Newcastle
and beyond. There was definitely a bit of romance
attached to the LNER that some people envied.
I always used to think it made no difference
– every company had great men and at least some
great engines, and that was the main thing.*

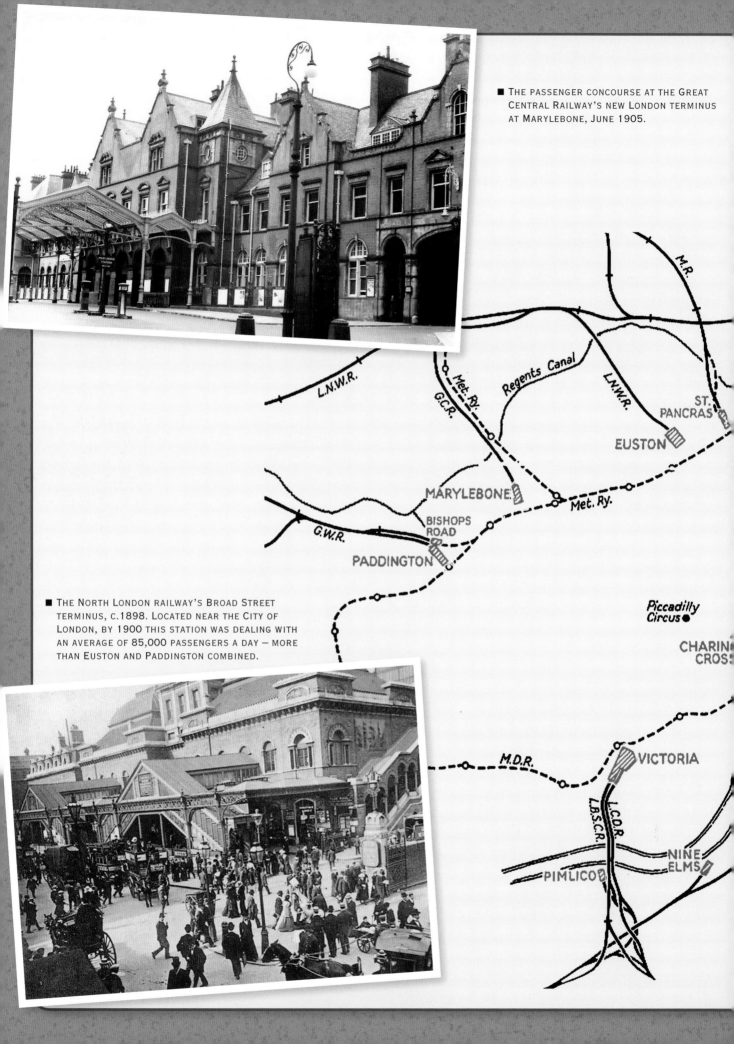

■ THE PASSENGER CONCOURSE AT THE GREAT
CENTRAL RAILWAY'S NEW LONDON TERMINUS
AT MARYLEBONE, JUNE 1905.

■ THE NORTH LONDON RAILWAY'S BROAD STREET
TERMINUS, C.1898. LOCATED NEAR THE CITY OF
LONDON, BY 1900 THIS STATION WAS DEALING WITH
AN AVERAGE OF 85,000 PASSENGERS A DAY — MORE
THAN EUSTON AND PADDINGTON COMBINED.

ALL ROADS LEAD TO LONDON

In London, the competition between rival railway companies did not result in simply more than one station as was the case in many cities around the country but in many grand termini, sometimes built almost on top of each other. Some of them still remain key hubs of the railways system but the importance of stations such as Broad Street, Bricklayer's Arms or Nine Elms is less well remembered.

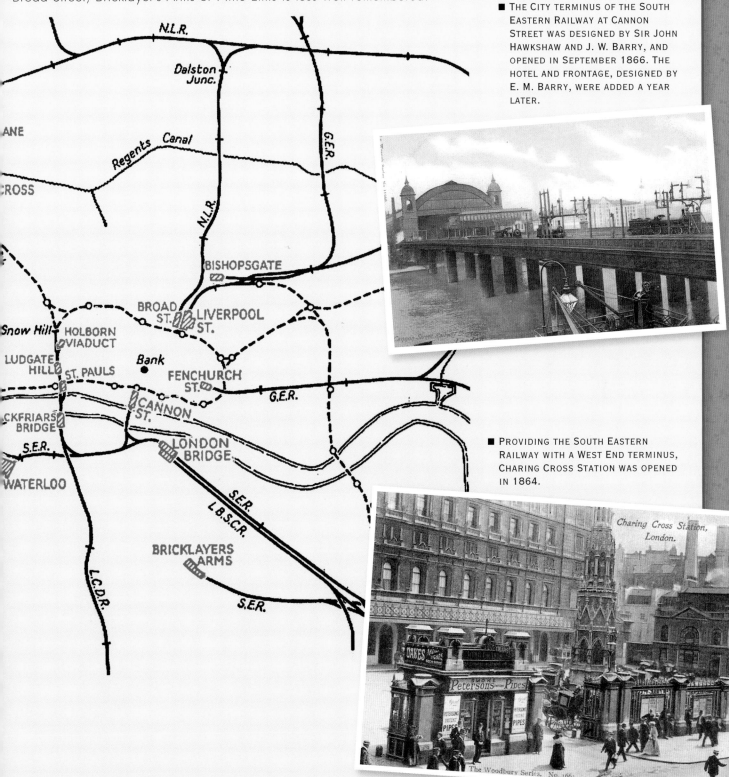

■ THE CITY TERMINUS OF THE SOUTH EASTERN RAILWAY AT CANNON STREET WAS DESIGNED BY SIR JOHN HAWKSHAW AND J. W. BARRY, AND OPENED IN SEPTEMBER 1866. THE HOTEL AND FRONTAGE, DESIGNED BY E. M. BARRY, WERE ADDED A YEAR LATER.

■ PROVIDING THE SOUTH EASTERN RAILWAY WITH A WEST END TERMINUS, CHARING CROSS STATION WAS OPENED IN 1864.

The Big Four: GWR

Of the big four companies, the most exalted reputation was that enjoyed by the Great Western Railway (GWR). As a major employer of the area it served, it bestowed enviable prestige on anyone who was in the pay of 'God's Wonderful Railway'.

Arthur Archer, who worked for more than 40 years on the GWR, recalled how Spartan railway life was in the 1930s and 1940s:

There were no canteens for guards or drivers and in the guards' room management would have thought it very bad for morale to provide comfortable chairs. We just had bare wooden benches – we got round the problem by bringing in our own chairs – some men brought in big old armchairs or they'd get an old leather seat that used to be used on the platform or in one of the passenger waiting rooms.

Arthur worked trains down to Bristol, Cardiff, Exeter, Banbury and Old Oak Common in west London. The area covered by the GWR was so extensive and its reputation such that GWR men could get financial credit almost anywhere, as Arthur recalled:

My father could get credit in London in the days when a Swindon bricklayer couldn't get credit in the shop at the corner of his street! And in Swindon you didn't ask a man what he did for a living – you asked him, 'Are you in or out?' Everyone knew that meant, do you work for the Great Western Railway or for someone else?

■ A BUSY SCENE AT PLATFORM 1 OF PADDINGTON STATION DURING THE 1930S, PRIOR TO THE DEPARTURE OF THE 'CORNISHMAN' EXPRESS.

■ Shed workers at Old Oak Common show great interest in the semi-streamlined Great Western 'King' Class 4-6-0 No.6014, 'King Henry VII'. In its air-smoothed form the locomotive was still something of a novelty in March 1935.

DIRECTORS' PERKS

GWR used to issue its directors – one of whom was the Prime Minister, Harold Macmillan – with a solid gold pass which allowed the bearer to travel free, First Class, anywhere on the rail network in Britain. This privilege was ended after the Second World War when GWR were absorbed into British Railways, but apparently Macmillan – a famously thrifty man – continued to use his pass until the end of his life. He would often have to give the BR official a potted history of the development of the railway system before being allowed to pass.

For a number of years after steam disappeared and the driver's life changed out of all recognition, the guard's life stayed pretty much the same – it was still the same old bloody van! But the design of the van differed between regions.

The Great Western Railway guard's van had a veranda at one end. Midland region vans had a veranda at both ends. The brake itself – an old-fashioned thing that you literally screwed down by turning a handle round and round – was slap-bang in the middle of the van. We had what we called a bubble on either side of the van, basically a small window. According to the rulebook you were supposed to remain alert and vigilant at all times, but once diesel came in we used to say that you were safer lying down on the floor with the guard's bag under your head. In the bag we'd have all our gear as well as tea, milk and sugar and something to eat – and of course you had your little stove so you could heat things up. It was easier doing it this way than frying your eggs on the shovel, which is what I used to do when I was firing.

'… in Swindon you didn't ask a man what he did for a living – you asked him, "Are you in or out?"'

■ This GWR outside-frame locomotive, 4-4-0 No.3378 'River Tawe', was in use in the 1930s.

The
BOX TUNNEL
BUILT BY
I.K.BRUNEL

COMMENCED 1836
OPENED
JUNE 30TH 1841

IT IS A REMARKABLE FACT THAT ANNUALLY ON THE MORNING OF APRIL 9TH, THE SUN'S RAYS PENETRATE THROUGH THE GREAT BOX TUNNEL OF THE GREAT WESTERN RAILWAY AND ON NO OTHER DAY IN THE YEAR.
THE DAILY TELEGRAPH. APRIL 12TH 1859
EVEN MORE REMARKABLE IS THE FACT THAT APRIL 9TH IS THE BIRTHDAY OF BRUNEL.

■ A ROMANTIC VIEW OF BRUNEL'S BOX TUNNEL ON THE BRISTOL TO PADDINGTON BROAD GAUGE LINE, WHICH WAS COMPLETED IN 1841.

■ GWR BROAD GAUGE 4-2-4T No.2002 WAS ORIGINALLY BUILT FOR THE BRISTOL & EXETER RAILWAY. PICTURED HERE AT SWINDON WORKS, THESE LOCOMOTIVES HAD 9FT DIAMETER DRIVING WHEELS.

Guards were always famous for having classy newspapers like The Times *and* The Observer *– they didn't read them, but they were just right for folding into strips to keep the draughts out of the van! The old-style guard and his van are now long gone, along with the amazing institutions and structure of the old Great Western. Would you believe it, but as well as running its own buses and coal mines and making every conceivable item necessary for railway work, the Great Western ran tests on everything – right down to the timber used in the coachwork.*

If you looked out the carriage window on one stretch of track near Wantage you used to see lots of wood panels on a hoarding – they were all left there, completely open to the elements, to test their durability. It was the perfect spot because not only did they have to put up with the weather, they also had all the steam and smuts from passing trains.

After retirement Arthur became the one-hundredth mayor of Swindon and he was also the last mayor who had worked for the old Great Western Railway. He recalls:

Well over half Swindon's mayors were railwaymen, but only the very old like me can still remember the days before British Rail, when the Great Western Railway was always known among the men by its nickname: God's Wonderful Railway.

Vinsun Gulliver, who was driving in the 1920s, recalled that even the coal could differ between regions:

On the LNER – which is where I moved later on in my career – I think it would be fair to say that our methods of locomotive practice were not as consistent as, say, those of the Great Western, but then they had much better coal!

Engineer Bill Sidwell remembered a key difference between his region and the GWR:

A lot of London Midland engines were very rough riding. Great Western engines were definitely better; they had a few shortcomings but no Great Western man would ever admit it or tell you what they were!

'... only the very old like me can still remember the days before British Rail'

■ OPENING DAY AT
CHEDDAR STATION ON
THE BROAD GAUGE
BRANCHLINE FROM
YATTON TO WITHAM, 3
AUGUST 1869.

Signalman Harry Horn recalled one of the GWR's greatest achievements:

The Automatic Train Control system (ATC) was invented in the Great Western region. That was a marvellous innovation, and it's now in use everywhere on the railways. It was such a simple idea – they installed small ramps between the rails so many yards from each distant signal. The ramps were attached to a battery and when the distant signal up ahead was at caution the ramp was electrified. If the train ignored the signal for whatever reason and ran over the ramp, a charge was sent up into the engine and this automatically applied the brakes. So if something terrible had happened to the driver the train would still stop before the next signal. Once the ATCs appeared in the Western Region every region wanted them – that's how good they are.

■ GWR 'CASTLE' CLASS
4-6-0 No.5054 'EARL
OF DUCIE' HEADS
THROUGH SEVERN
TUNNEL JUNCTION
WITH A SOUTH WALES
EXPRESS IN THE
1930S.

But perhaps the final word about the Great Western should go to Arthur Archer in Swindon:

The Great Western Railway made everything – engines, wheels, pistons, coaches and carriage cloth. We also made our own soap, pins, grease, furniture – everything. We ran our own buses, foundries and even coal mines. The GWR was self-governing and self-sufficient – far more influential than the town council.

The Big Four: LMS

The big four railway companies tried to promote themselves in ways that can seem remarkably outward-looking and modern – the London, Midland and Scottish railway (LMS), for example, offered a range of travel films for hire to the general public and they promoted further education classes for their workers.

Sandy Begg recalled:

I was passed for driving on the LMS in 1958 but years before, when I was a cleaner, I made sure I went to the local improvement classes. They were really part of my social life, apart from all the other benefits. Mind you, we were so busy most of the time that it was tiring to go on to classes after work at all.

At St Margaret's in Edinburgh, for example, there were over a thousand footplate staff – can you believe that? Yet despite these large numbers the men were so busy that their engines were kept almost continually fired up. Three shifts every 24 hours kept drivers and firemen permanently on the go.

Mostly we used three-cylinder K3 engines (LMS men called them Moguls). We also had V2s, Green Arrows and J37s with old Stephenson link gears. The J36s we used were called Ypres or Mons Meg because they'd been used in the Great War. Firing was different according to the engine you were on – each had a different-sized firebox. For a start, older engines had very deep fire-boxes; this was because they always used cheap coal from the Lothians and you needed a lot of it to get sufficient heat. The engines used for the north east runs had shallower fireboxes because they used superior coal from Yorkshire.

SMALL MARGINS

In 1938, the LMS operated around 6,870 route miles (11,056 km) of railway (excluding its lines in Northern Ireland), but it was not said to be very profitable, with a rate of return of only 2.7%. The main trunk routes were the West Coast Main Line and the Midland Main Line, linking London, the industrial Midlands and North-West of England, and Scotland. The railway's main business was the transport of freight between these major industrial centres.

■ STANIER 'PRINCESS ROYAL' CLASS
4-6-2 NO. 6203 'PRINCESS
MARGARET ROSE' STANDS AT
PLATFORM 2 AT EUSTON STATION
IN THE 1930S.

■ STANIER 'PRINCESS CORONATION'
CLASS 4-6-2 PACIFIC NO.6232,
'DUCHESS OF MONTROSE' STANDS
IN MAGNIFICENT LMS CRIMSON
LIVERY AT SHREWSBURY STATION
IN JUNE 1938.

*'... the men were
so busy that their
engines were kept
almost continually
fired up'*

- Ex-London & North Western Railway 'Precursor' Class 4-4-0 No.25319 (above) simmers away at the platform at Coventry in May 1939.

- Ex-MR Class '4P' 2-6-4T No.2328 (right) at St Albans City station in May 1939.

- Former Midland Railway Class '2P' 4-4-0 No.366 (below), seen here in LMS livery.

According to Sandy, firemen and drivers were experts on coal and could spot the good from the bad in a second:

I recall one old driver called Jimmy Allen, who was normally a quiet bloke, looking with disgust at a particularly dreadful batch of coal. He took a great big lump of it and took it to the engineer's desk, plonked it down on his desk in front of him and said, 'See if that'll burn in your fire – it won't burn in mine!'

Driver Vinsun Gulliver, who retired in the 1950s having worked for both the LNER and LMS, recalled:

*I remember I cleaned the **Queen Alexander** – one of our few special engines – and it was a magnificent thing because most of our local LMS engines didn't have names, they were just engines used for the local passenger and goods trains. I think the LMS reputation was solid but unglamorous – although the GWR boys thought we were rubbish!*

'... the LMS reputation was solid but unglamorous – although the GWR boys thought we were rubbish!'

■ A WARTIME VIEW AT THE NORTH END OF YORK STATION (LEFT). CLASS 'A4' 4-6-2 No.4499, 'SIR MURROUGH WILSON', PULLS A NORTHBOUND TRAIN, WHILE A GRIMY CLASS 'V2' 2-6-2 HEADS SOUTH, UNDER THE WATCHFUL EYE OF A YOUNG SPOTTER.

■ A SCHOOLBOY ENTHUSIAST (LEFT) CHECKS AN IMPRESSIVE LINE UP AT KING'S CROSS DEPOT IN THE 1950S WITH THREE 'A4'S AND TWO 'A3'S IN EVIDENCE. FROM THE LEFT THEY ARE, AN UNIDENTIFIED GRESLEY 'A4' PACIFIC; 'A4' No.60014, 'SILVER LINK' CARRYING THE 'FLYING SCOTSMAN' HEADBOARD; FELLOW 'A4' No.60025, 'FALCON' COMPLETE WITH 'THE ELIZABETHAN' HEADBOARD; GRESLEY 'A3' PACIFIC No.60059, 'TRACERY' AND COMPLETING THE LINE UP AND THE SUBJECT OF THE YOUNG ENTHUSIASTS' ATTENTION, 'A3' No.60037, 'HYPERION' A HAYMARKET ENGINE AND SOMETHING OF A RARITY AT KINGS CROSS.

TRAINSPOTTING

A glimpse of one of the great locomotives in action was an experience of pure excitement – a thrill that few dedicated trainspotters ever entirely grew out of.

■ THE JOYS OF TRAIN SPOTTING IN A SYLVAN SETTING (LEFT), AS A GREAT WESTERN RAILWAY EXPRESS PASSES, HAULED BY AN UNIDENTIFIED 'SAINT' CLASS 4-6-0, C1930.

■ SEEN HERE ON 18 AUGUST 1962, THE MURKY DEPTHS OF BIRMINGHAM NEW STREET (BELOW) STILL ATTRACTED ITS FAIR SHARE OF YOUNG SPOTTERS.

■ SCHOOLBOY TRAINSPOTTERS WITH A GOOD VIEW OF THE ACTION AT NEWCASTLE-UPON-TYNE STATION, AUGUST 1960.

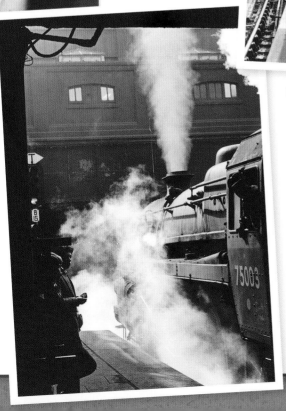

■ TRAINSPOTTERS EXAMINE THE BR STANDARD CLASS '4MT' 4-6-0 NO.75003 AS IT WAITS TO DEPART FROM BIRMINGHAM SNOW HILL WITH THE 10.20 TO RAMSGATE AND MARGATE IN AUGUST 1962.

■ A YOUNG ENTHUSIAST TEMPORARILY DISTRACTED FROM THE LOADING OF MAIL IN RURAL IRELAND, 1955.

■ RESPLENDENT IN NEW LIVERY, SOUTHERN RAILWAY H15 CLASS 4-6-0 No.483 STANDS OUTSIDE EASTLEIGH WORKS IN APRIL 1938.

■ THE SHORT-LIVED 'KENTISH BELLE' PULLMAN EXPRESS (BELOW) — LATER KNOWN AS THE 'THANET BELLE' — SEEN HERE HAULED BY 'KING ARTHUR' CLASS 4-6-0 No.30763, 'SIR BORS DE GANIS'.

The Big Four: SR

The big four regions each had their own characters and they inspired intense loyalty in those who worked for them.

Shedmaster Richard Hardy experienced life on the LNER and on the Southern Railway (SR), as he remembered:

After a little over two years at Ipswich, I found myself posted to Stewarts Lane, Battersea, in South London. This was very different from Ipswich. Here, on the Southern Region, punctuality was a religion.

Our drivers were accountable for every minute lost and I was accountable to my chief. If a driver lost two minutes from Victoria to Herne Hill after a tough time climbing the grade out of Victoria, he would no doubt regain it by Tonbridge, but the two minutes went down against Stewarts Lane and that really upset everyone involved.

There were two punctuality leagues that were judged according to minutes lost per 1,000 miles run. We were always well up the first division, but never at the top because of the complexity of the services our men handled. It was a splendid discipline, but administratively, it cost a lot of money, especially as any time loss disputed had to be settled and any delays were pursued so that there would be no repetition by those responsible – which usually included the chap in charge (ie me) and rightly so! Woodford and Ipswich were positively gentlemanly compared with those tough, uncompromising Battersea boys!

Of all the wonderful jobs I had, Stewarts Lane brought me nearest to the real running of the railway. Some 750 south London boys, most of them outspoken and critical of management, would nevertheless rise to the occasion to meet the demands of the summer service year after year. It was a remarkable job, hard work, seven days a week, a fortnight's holiday a year.

When I needed a break, I would go down to Dover on the engine of the Golden Arrow, maybe do the driving on the down and the firing on the up road, and that put me right again. At Stewarts Lane, you had to be the guvn'r: if you were easy, you were finished; the Cockneys had no respect for an easy boss. You had to be fair and straight so we had our battles, but they were good-hearted battles with no grudges held.

'Here, on the Southern Region, punctuality was a religion'

■ SOUTHERN RAILWAY 'MERCHANT NAVY' CLASS 4-6-2 NO.21C11 'GENERAL STEAM NAVIGATION' HURTLES THROUGH CLAPHAM JUNCTION IN AUGUST 1947 WITH THE DOWN 'DEVON BELLE' PULLMAN TRAIN.

■ A 1930s SOUTHERN RAILWAY POSTER FOR THE 'BOURNEMOUTH BELLE', SHOWN HERE BEING HAULED BY A STYLISED 'LORD NELSON' CLASS 4-6-0.

SOUTHERN · RAILWAY

58

Nº 862

BOURNEMOUTH BELLE
RUNS·DAILY.

KENTISH BELLE

475

'... the foreman on the Southern at Battersea was a fussy bugger.'

■ TWO STIRLING CLASS 'R1' 0-6-0TS, NOS.1337 AND 1174, PULLING A CONTINENTAL EXPRESS FROM FOLKESTONE HARBOUR. A THIRD 0-6-0T WOULD BE BANKING AT THE REAR.

Reg Coote worked on the Southern Railway during the War, a time when many of the old traditions had to be changed to meet the needs of a uniquely difficult time, as he recalled:

The little group of lads I started work with at the Battersea depot in 1941 were the lowest of the low. Grease monkeys we were. All we did was clean the engines, the dirtiest job you can imagine. We were all 16 or 17 and as we trooped around the shed I always went first, carrying the board that said 'Cleaning in progress' as if it was a military flag, and followed by a lad carrying the oil in what we called a bottle (the oil smelled like cat's pee!); the next lad in the line carried the Vaseline for cleaning and someone else had the cotton waste, the wipes and rags we would use. The cleaner foreman showed us how to clean, because it wasn't that straightforward and it had to be just right. Passenger engines had to be knobbed up a good bit more than goods but they all had to pass the foreman's test – and the foreman on the Southern at Battersea was a fussy bugger. He'd come along and check underneath in all those little inaccessible places you might have thought you could get away with not cleaning at all.

We used pumice and brick dust to make the metalwork shine but sometimes the metalwork was too awful to do much with, however hard we tried. Take the 21C – the first Merchant Navy class. I remember cleaning that engine at the end of 1941 and the paintwork was so rough it shredded our rags – absolutely tore them to bits! Most engines on the Southern were in a right state during the war, because there was no time and no money to keep up standards.

Within six weeks of us starting work we were told: 'You're going out as firemen.' Proud as Punch, we immediately went round scrounging caps from older firemen, but I think they bloody hated it! They'd spent years working their way up and we came along and got the same jobs in five minutes!

■ THE 'DEVON BELLE' PULLMAN EXPRESS, HEADED BY BULLEID 'MERCHANT NAVY' CLASS 4-6-2 NO.35007 "ABERDEEN COMMONWEALTH", STANDS READY TO DEPART FROM EXETER CENTRAL IN 1947.

On Private Lines

Here and there throughout the railway network there were curious stretches of private railway. One or two landowners – including a Victorian Scottish earl – had paid for the line to be extended over their land, but businesses were often the inspiration for short stretches of private line.

'... the railways could survive in small, out-of-the-way places, but only if they cooperated with local businesses'

Lowestoft stationmaster Rod Lock remembered a typical example:

At East Winch, much of the freight was agricultural produce, particularly grain, because we were in one of the most important agricultural areas of England. In my day the railways carried more than 300 million tons of freight a year, whereas only a fraction of that was being carried by the time I retired.

The local agricultural firm actually had a private siding at East Winch – that's how important their business was to us. The firm was called Bull and Northcott – day in and day out their grain was forwarded to us at the rate of about two or three wagon-loads a day. That's a lot of produce, and if you multiply that by all the thousands of tiny rural stations up and down the country doing similar levels of business you can see why the railways could survive in small, out-of-the-way places, but only if they cooperated with local businesses.

Cliff Carr, working at Walcot in Herefordshire, was nominally in charge of a private stretch of railway that ran into the works of one of the region's biggest employers – British Sugar:

The sugar-beet industry was so important in the area around Walcot that the stationmaster – ie me! – even had an office in the British Sugar Corporation factory at nearby Allscott at the end of their private line.

I'm pretty sure that arrangement – a stationmaster at work in a sugar factory – was unique in British Railways, but it made sense as we had sidings there and so much of our business depended on the factory and close liaison with the factory manager and the endless freight that came to us.

■ EAST KENT RAILWAY 0-6-0 SADDLE TANK NO.2 IN THE 1930S (TOP). FORMERLY ONE OF COLONEL STEPHENS'S LIGHT RAILWAYS, THE EKR SERVED COAL MINES IN KENT AND BECAME PART OF BRITISH RAILWAYS IN 1948. BY 1951 MOST OF THE RAILWAY HAD BEEN CLOSED.

■ A 2FT 6IN GAUGE WELSHPOOL & LLANFAIR LIGHT RAILWAY FREIGHT TRAIN (LEFT) HAULED BY 0-6-0T NO.822. FROM ITS OPENING IN 1903, THE W&L WAS OPERATED BY CAMBRIAN RAILWAYS UNTIL ABSORBED INTO THE GWR IN 1922. PASSENGER TRAFFIC CEASED IN 1931 BUT GOODS TRAFFIC CONTINUED THROUGH NATIONALIZATION IN 1948 UNTIL CLOSURE BY BR IN 1956.

A FINAL JOURNEY

Brookwood cemetery in Surrey was the unusual site for a private line – built in the 1850s to transport coffins and mourners from London, 25 miles away. A private terminus just outside Waterloo was linked to two private stations in the cemetery and although services ceased permanently during the Second World War, the last of the stations survived until the 1970s and the trackbed may still be followed through the grounds today.

■ THE WESTON, CLEVEDON & PORTISHEAD RAILWAY WAS ALSO PART OF THE COLONEL STEPHENS RAILWAY EMPIRE. THE LINE CLOSED IN 1940.

RECORD BREAKERS

The fastest running machines on earth – famous locomotives once had an aura comparable to that enojyed by jet fighters and sleek new airliners today.

■ THE GWR'S 4-4-0 'CITY OF TRURO' ACHIEVED 100MPH DOWN WELLINGTON BANK BETWEEN TAUNTON AND EXETER IN 1904.

■ LONDON & NORTH EASTERN RAILWAY CLASS 'A3' 4-6-2 NO.2750 'PAPYRUS', SHOWN HERE AT KINGS CROSS SHED, WAS BUILT IN 1929 AND BEARS THE 'SCARBOROUGH FLYER' HEADBOARD. THIS ENGINE ACHIEVED FAME IN MARCH 1935 WHEN IT MADE HIGH SPEED RUNS BETWEEN KINGS CROSS AND NEWCASTLE IN 3 HOURS 47 1/2 MINUTES, SO PAVING THE WAY FOR THE LNER'S FIRST STREAMLINED EXPRESS 'SILVER JUBILEE' LATER THAT YEAR.

■ Streamlined LMS Stanier Pacific No.6220, 'Coronation' stands ready to depart from London Euston with the 'Coronation Scot' in 1937. This locomotive achieved 114mph on a test train near Crewe in the same year.

■ The holder of the world record for steam traction, ex-LNER Gresley Class 'A4' 4-6-2 'Mallard', carrying BR No.60022, simmers gently whilst standing with a train at Kings Cross, c1958.

"The CORONATION"
THE FIRST STREAMLINE TRAIN
KING'S CROSS FOR SCOTLAND

DOMINION OF CANADA

LONDON & NORTH EASTERN RAILWAY

■ Stylized LNER poster for its streamlined 'Coronation' express, hauled by Gresley's 'A4' Pacifics, which was introduced between King's Cross and Edinburgh in 1935.

Bombing of Trains and Stations

The railways were key to Britain's survival during the war. Without trains there would be no troop movements, food or fuel distribution. The Germans knew this and constantly targeted the railways, particularly where they ran close to industrial centres and right across the south east.

Reg Coote recalled the terrors of wartime driving:

Many railwaymen were killed during German air raids and important railway offices sometimes had their headquarters inside tunnels. The tunnels were useful in other ways, too – if a train was buzzed by enemy aircraft the driver and firemen would race for the nearest tunnel, as I did on a number of occasions. Once, we reached the tunnel only just in time and a bomb missed us by a few dozen yards.

Signalman George Case recalled that for railwaymen living near the line as he did bombs were a constant threat:

It was February 26, 1941 – I can remember the exact date – and late that evening our next door neighbour came round and asked us to join her. My Dad had told my Mum not to leave the house whatever happened because his theory was that if a bomb was going to get you it would get you wherever you were, so you might as well stay in the house. So my Mum said no and we stayed put. A short while later our neighbour came in again – she was upset and asked us again to join her. I think she just wanted company. Anyway, Mum again refused and she stuck to her guns until the neighbour became hysterical. At last we relented and trooped into next door. A short while later our house took a direct hit and there's no doubt at all that if we'd stayed put we'd have all been killed. As it was they just had to dig us out!

There was a lot of bombing in the Potters Bar area because there were three railway tunnels close by – the Germans knew they would cause huge disruption if they managed to damage any of them.

At the Holloway signalbox George and his signalman would frequently receive what was called a London Central Yellow warning if enemy bombers were known to be in the area during the day. A London Central Red meant the bombers were now really close.

■ PREVIOUS PAGE: CHILDREN BEING EVACUATED FROM LONDON DURING THE BLITZ IN WORLD WAR II.

■ EXTENSIVE DAMAGE WAS CAUSED BY THE EXPLOSION OF A LAND MINE AT PADDINGTON STATION, LONDON IN APRIL 1941.

■ BOMB DAMAGE AT ST PANCRAS STATION, LONDON, 1940.

■ PREVIOUS PAGE: CHILDREN BEING EVACUATED FROM LONDON DURING THE BLITZ IN WORLD WAR II.

'Once, we reached the tunnel only just in time and a bomb missed us by a few dozen yards'

'When we came out from under the table we noticed that the huge beams that held up the roof had shifted about half an inch'

■ SERIOUS BOMB DAMAGE WAS INFLICTED ON PLATFORMS 1, 2 AND 3 AT YORK STATION ON 29 APRIL 1942.

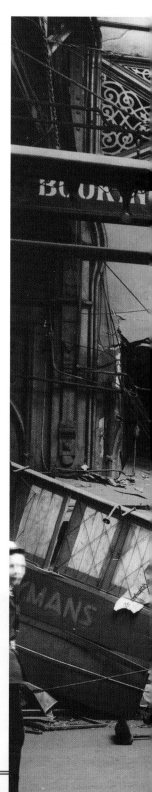

Sometimes I wondered why they bothered to warn us, since there was nothing we could do. We just sat there like sitting targets and dimmed our lights a bit. It was mainly gas lights in those days so they were pretty dim anyway and all the windows were blacked out with a hole left just big enough for the signalman to look out and peer up and down the line.

In the back of the cabin at Holloway they fitted a big steel shelter – actually inside the cabin. Old Dusty, my boss, used to get nervy when there were bombers about so he'd go into the shelter at the back of the box and tell me to get on with it.

Before he left school and through the last years of the war driver David Lubbock would see the bomb-carrying trains pass close to his Norfolk village on their way to the big American bases. He watched a German air attack on the railway junction at Melton Constable a few miles away:

I can remember they hit the water tanks at the rail junction there – the damage was terrible. The Germans were always trying to disrupt the rails to stop us moving things round the country. But it was a funny thing – we saw that bomber get shot down and it turned out that the German pilot had been chosen for the mission because he'd gone to school in Norfolk and he knew it like the back of his hand!

Driver Fred Simpson, based in Swindon, had similar wartime experiences:

Surprisingly we didn't suffer that much from German bombs. All I can remember was a big one coming down in Ferndale Road, just down the road from where I live. It was close to Running Shed No. 1, where we were all hanging around waiting to start work. We were in what we called the cabin, under a table, when the bomb hit and I can remember the ground shaking violently. When we came out from under the table we noticed that the huge beams that held up the roof had shifted about half an inch. They'd lifted when the bomb exploded and then re-settled. Apart from that there was no damage.

The only other incident I can recall was one night when I was out chatting to my neighbour at the end of the front garden. A German plane came in low towards us and strafed us with its machine gun. Luckily he missed but I picked up one of the bullets and I still have it!

■ BOMB DAMAGE AT LONDON PADDINGTON'S POST OFFICE AND BOOKING OFFICE DURING THE BLITZ IN WORLD WAR II.

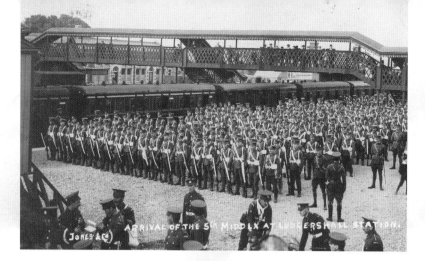

'We also used to move trains
around a lot to keep the
Germans guessing.'

■ ARRIVAL OF THE 5TH
MIDDLESEX REGIMENT
AT LUDGERSHALL
STATION DURING
WORLD WAR I.

Men at Arms

Throughout the war soldiers and their equipment had to be carried across the country and to the Channel ports.

Troop transport had its scary moments, but also its lighter side, as driver Reg Coote recalled:
I worked with a driver called Bill Murray during the war years – a great character – and once when we were heading for Brighton we were buzzed by a German plane. We were in the second engine of a double-header and you've never seen anything like the spurt we put on – despite the weight of a hell of a lot of carriages – to get to the nearest tunnel. We suddenly found we had the strength of ten men – that's what fear does to you! Anyway, we waited hours in the tunnel till we thought it was safe to come out and finally arrived in Brighton at 4am. We were taking a load of Scottish troops to the coast and when they marched out of the station at 4am I've always wondered what the locals made of the fact that the troops insisted on a full pipe band playing full blast at the head of the column!

■ US ARMY
TRANSPORTATION
CORPS CLASS 'S160'
2-8-0 No.1712 WITH
A FREIGHT TRAIN AT
BISHOPS STORTFORD
IN AUGUST 1943.

Reg also remembered driving ammunition trains:

There were loads of them as well as troop trains and tank trains. The tank trains were interesting. They'd be made up as follows: you'd get two locomotives one behind the other at the front (you'd need that sort of power because of the weight of the tanks) followed by a coach for the officers, then a coach for the men, then flat beds for the tanks, then another coach.

We also used to move trains around a lot to keep the Germans guessing. I can recall a couple of these trains made up with each flat bed loaded with giant papier mâché guns – from the air the idea was that the Germans would think we were incredibly well equipped when the opposite was true.

The railway helped with some great tricks in the war – down at Dover we had one massive gun, a real one this time, mounted on the railway. This was used to lob shells regularly over the Channel. When it fired it would quickly reverse through a long tunnel, pop out the other side and fire again, so old Gerry thought we had two big guns there, not just one!

At a time when Britain's population was suffering from severe shortages of everything from clothing to food, the railwayman's lot could occasionally be a happy one and never more so than when well-fed American troops began to arrive. As driver Fred Simpson recalled:

When the Yanks first came over we had to move them around the country and as soon as we'd dropped a load of them off, we used to go straight into the carriages to collect up the ration boxes they always left all over the place. The boxes each contained one meal for a man, together with chewing gum, chocolate and even condoms! The chocolate was horrible, but to us poor half-starved devils the fact that most of the boxes were left untouched was a wonderful bonus.

■ THIS MEMORIAL WAS
ERECTED BY THE
LONDON & NORTH
WESTERN RAILWAY
IN MEMORY OF ITS
RAILWAYMEN WHO WERE
KILLED DURING WORLD
WAR I.

■ MEMORIAL NEXT TO THE CITY WALLS IN
YORK TO THE LNER RAILWAY WORKERS
KILLED IN BOTH WORLD WARS.

■ MEMORIAL AT LONDON, VICTORIA STATION TO
THE LONDON BRIGHTON AND SOUTH COAST
RAILWAY EMPLOYEES KILLED IN WORLD WAR I.

WAR MEMORIALS

Railway workers did their bit during the war – whether they had restricted jobs and remained on the railways or were called up. Countless memorials at stations up and down the country testify to their bravery and sacrifice.

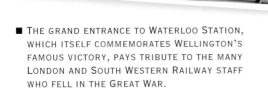

■ THE GRAND ENTRANCE TO WATERLOO STATION, WHICH ITSELF COMMEMORATES WELLINGTON'S FAMOUS VICTORY, PAYS TRIBUTE TO THE MANY LONDON AND SOUTH WESTERN RAILWAY STAFF WHO FELL IN THE GREAT WAR.

■ THE 'ROLL OF HONOUR' OF GWR EMPLOYEES WHO DIED IN WORLD WAR I RECORDED ON A FRAMED PRINT AT EXETER ST DAVID'S STATION.

3312
MEN AND WOMEN
OF THE
GREAT WESTERN RAILWAY
GAVE THEIR LIVES
FOR KING AND COUNTRY

■ A POIGNANT STATUE AT PADDINGTON STATION ERECTED IN MEMORY OF 3,312 GWR EMPLOYEES WHO DIED IN WORLD WAR I.

Evacuees

Among the most poignant images in British history are those black and white photographs of long lines of bewildered children waiting at city stations across the country during the Second World War. They were waiting to leave cities that were about to be or had already been bombed.

Most went to live in the countryside with strangers or family, but others went overseas, sometimes for years, and the shock of parting stayed with them forever. Ruth Maltby recalled her journey from Portsmouth to Liverpool, where she took ship for Canada:

I went with my mother, father and brother; first to London and then from Euston to Liverpool. I remember being afraid at the noise and chaos of so many people milling around – the train was dark and dirty and we sped through unlit tunnels. It was summer, but raining, misty and miserable. There were soldiers on the train, I recall, as well as other children and every station we passed through had its name blacked out – the idea was to eliminate anything and everything that could help the enemy.

■ EVACUEE CHILDREN, PICTURED HERE AT THE STATION, PREPARING TO LEAVE BOMB-TORN LONDON FOR THE SAFETY OF THE COUNTRYSIDE IN 1939.

I had to be pulled on to the train because like many children I was reluctant to go. They took our gas masks off us when we got on the train. I remember the windows that could only be opened by pulling a leather strap that had holes in it for different heights. We had to close them each time we went through a tunnel or the carriage would fill with smoke.

One odd thing that was very different from today was that despite the noise and clutter there was no rubbish on the floor of the train nor on the platforms.

The whole thing was such a shock to a child – we weren't allowed to ask questions and couldn't take any toys or books. I only had my paintbox. There seemed to be so many railway officials everywhere. Train guards monitored everything extremely closely – checking tickets, walking through the carriages at frequent intervals.

As we left London I saw the grimy backs of houses and the tiny grey gardens, then factories and at last the countryside, but hardly any cars because of the petrol rationing. Liverpool, which we reached six hours after leaving Euston, was just as smoky and dark as London, but there were plenty of porters to carry our cases. They seemed to be glad of the work and the tips. And then I boarded the ship and left England. It was more than two years before I was able to return.

In Cheshire, Harry Horn, by now a driver, also remembered child evacuees:

I can remember the Friday before war was declared. We took a GC Pom Pom to Skelton Junction turntable, where we were to back on to a passenger special. It was a lovely sunny day and we took that passenger special to Liverpool to pick up evacuated children. I can see them vividly now: they all had gas masks and they all looked so alone and so sad. I was told later by the guard that whereas a train filled with children would usually be full of shouts and laughter that evacuee train was eerily quiet. It made you realize the effect the horrible disruption was having on the children.

■ A GROUP OF 317 EVACUEE CHILDREN WAIT AT A RAILWAY STATION IN LIVERPOOL BEFORE TRAVELLING TO SAFER AREAS, 27TH AUGUST 1942.

■ TWO POLICEWOMEN AND A VAD (VOLUNTARY AID DETACHMENT) NURSE SERVE REFRESHMENTS TO THE YOUNG EVACUEES BEFORE THEIR DEPARTURE FROM LONDON TO THE COMPARATIVE SAFETY OF THE COUNTRYSIDE DURING WORLD WAR II, JUNE 1940.

143

BRITISH RAILWAYS

Widespread enthusiasm greeted the nationalization of the rail network after the war, but the new system brought problems of its own.

Building a New Britain

The railways were nationalized at a time when the prevailing view in Britain – a view held by the left and to a lesser though still significant extent by the right – was that something as important as the transport infrastructure should not be subject to the profit motive. People looked back at what the profit motive had done during the Great Depression of the 1930s and hoped that nationalization would usher in a brave new world.

Tom Shackle recalled the political background to nationalization:

Well, nationalization wasn't the dirty word it became during Mrs Thatcher's years in government. In the run up to 1948 there was surprisingly widespread support across all political parties for nationalization and not just of the railway – all the big commercial interests like road haulage, electricity, coal and gas were nationalized because it was felt to be in the national interest to take them out of private hands to protect the public. It was felt that private owners only cared about their shareholders and would do anything to increase shareholder dividends. In the 1940s I can remember we all felt that was selfish and immoral.

It's funny, isn't it, because only 30 years later that view had changed completely – the huge inefficiency and cumbersome bureaucracy of big state-owned industries made private enterprise seem almost virtuous. All these things are cyclical – after nationalization privatization seems refreshing and responsive, but then when we've had privatization too long we see that the profit motive can be terrible. Most recently we've seen what privatization means when private companies are paid to repair tracks: they do a bad job because they are trying to cut costs to the minimum, and then passengers die in terrible accidents.

■ POSTERS GO UP
IN DECEMBER
1947 INFORMING
PASSENGERS OF THE
END OF AN ERA.

■ THE NEW BRITISH
RAILWAYS LOGO
IS APPLIED TO A
LOCOMOTIVE IN
JANUARY 1948.

■ ATTLEE'S NEW LABOUR
GOVERNMENT TOOK
OFFICE IN 1945
WITH AN AMBITIOUS
AGENDA OF REFORMS,
INCLUDING THE
NATIONALIZATION OF
THE RAILWAYS. HERE
THE NEW PM SHARES
A JOKE WITH ERNEST
BEVIN AND HERBERT
MORRISON.

'It was felt that private owners only cared about their shareholders and would do anything to increase shareholder dividend'

Back in the 1940s socialism still seemed a positive experiment. The railways had been privately run during the 1930s and early 1940s, and what had been the result? – Run-down engines and track, shabby carriages and the Depression. People and politicians saw in nationalization a way to solve the problem of run-down railways and companies indulging in wasteful competition and duplication just to produce bigger dividends for their shareholders.

Labour's election in 1945 was very much a green light for nationalization because it had been a central plank of the party's campaign, and the old Tory-dominated wartime coalition was badly tainted by the war and all that the war meant. But even the Tories were not against nationalization and railway nationalization went ahead almost unopposed, except by the old railway owners, who used their influence in high places – the Lords and the City – to ensure that their shareholders received far higher compensation than they deserved. They were compensated for a railway network in tip-top condition, whereas the network was actually in a terrible state – deliberately neglected by the private owners. It's just sad that nationalization was eventually to have as many problems as privatization – they were just different problems!

Early Days

When the railways were nationalized on 1 January 1948 no one really had any idea how difficult it would be to turn around an industry previously split into four. They also had no idea how difficult it would be to sort out the chronic under-investment of the previous 30 or more years.

Tom Shackle recalled just a few of the difficulties:

Well it wasn't as bad as it became during the days of British Rail in the 1960s when the disgusting British Railway sandwich became a byword for failure, but it was bad. If memory serves I believe that the new British Railways was controlled by the British Transport Commission – an incredibly silly decision because the Commission was too big already: it looked after road haulage, the ports and the canals, which were still used for some transport. Far too big and therefore inefficient and chaotic. There was a Railway Executive as well I think, but no one knew who was really in charge.

■ SOME NEW ENGINES WERE INTRODUCED (RIGHT), LIKE THE HAWKSWORTH 'COUNTY' CLASS 4-6-0 No.1014 'COUNTY OF GLAMORGAN', SHOWN HERE AT BRISTOL TEMPLE MEADS ON 14 JUNE 1948, BUT IT WAS GENERALLY FELT THAT THE REORGANIZATION BROUGHT A DECLINE IN STANDARDS.

'… we'd got so used to things being difficult and dirty because of the war that we just accepted it, I suppose'

■ 'CASTLE' CLASS 4-6-0 NO.7015 'CARN BREA CASTLE' (LEFT) TACKLES HEMERDON BANK IN SOUTH DEVON WITH A TRAIN OF EASTERN REGION STOCK ON 6 AUGUST 1956.

■ INTRODUCED IN 1948, THE SCAMMELL 'MECHANICAL HORSES' (BELOW) LACKED THE APPEAL OF THE TRADITIONAL RAILWAY HORSE-DRAWN DELIVERY DRAYS WHICH THEY REPLACED.

Also, as with the more recent privatization, it was impossible in 1948 to know if the future would be better than the past because it was completely uncharted territory – one company had never run the railways. Also the Executive was bound to fail because the most senior railway bosses of the past effectively boycotted the new system because they'd been against it in the first place. And all this mess did filter down to how it felt to be a passenger.

Anne Scott agreed:

'm sure the trains were much slower and more often delayed after nationalization than before, but to be fair that was probably partly because of the damage done by the war to signals, track and so on. Also we knew that money wasn't being spent, as the carriages were dirtier and scruffier than they'd been in the 1930s and earlier, but then no one had any money. Our houses were scruffy too! And we'd got so used to things being difficult and dirty because of the war that we just accepted it, I suppose.

NEW TRAINS
Between 1948 and1960 British Railways built 2,537 steam locomotives. Of these, 1,538 were pre-nationalisation designs and 999 were standard designs. These locos had relatively short lives however, some as short as five years (they were designed to last over 30 years), due to the end of steam traction in 1968.

BR STEAM TRAINS

During the 1950s and 1960s one of British Railways' strategies to entice passengers to travel was to run named trains, adding new, glamourously titled services to the established famous trains such as 'The Flying Scotsman'.

■ REBUILT EX-SR 'MERCHANT NAVY' CLASS 4-6-2 NO.35018 'BRITISH INDIA LINE' HALTS AT SALISBURY WITH THE DOWN 'ATLANTIC COAST EXPRESS' ON 7 SEPTEMBER 1961.

■ EX-GWR 'CASTLE' CLASS 4-6-0 NO.5031 'TOTNES CASTLE' (LEFT) STORMS OUT OF GLOUCESTER EASTGATE WITH THE DOWN 'CORNISHMAN' ON 12 OCTOBER 1961.

■ Adorned with the headboard for the 'Cambrian Coast Express', ex-GWR 'Manor' Class 4-6-0 No.7819 'Hinton Manor' awaits departure from Shrewsbury Station on 30 May 1963.

■ Ex-LMS Stanier 4-6-2 No.46221, 'Queen Elizabeth' (below) speeds non-stop through Crewe with the up 'Royal Scot', much to the delight of the assembled train spotters on the platform, c1960.

All Pulling Together – The Move to Standardization

The rich variety of engines and rolling stock across the railway network was a source of endless fascination to enthusiasts, but standardization was the inevitable price paid in the move towards greater efficiency that came with nationalization.

Even before standardization proper there were attempts to create consistency across the various regions, at least in some respects, as shedmaster Richard Hardy recalled:

I was so lucky to be involved in so many areas of railway working and in many instances there was a sense that standardization was important. I can recall a fascinating meeting early in my career with the chief mechanical engineer for the LNER, Edward Thompson.

I had been interviewed by Mr Thompson when I left school and he had taken an interest in my progress. Early in 1942, in the dark at Wakefield Station, he spotted me getting off an engine and asked me what I was doing so late on a Saturday evening. The fact that I was learning to fire pleased him greatly, even though it was highly unofficial! When the train for Doncaster ran in, he beckoned me to follow, sat me down in a compartment and then told me about his plans for building new locomotives – the B1, the L1, his Pacifics, rebuilt K1s, B17s and, of course, the splendid O4 rebuild, to become the even better O1. Not all his engines were to be perfect but most were splendid jobs. He aimed to reduce the number of classes, to ease the lot of the running sheds by simplification and standardization and, given the appalling wartime shortages of material, his short reign of five and a half years was memorable.

■ ONE OF THE NEW STANDARDIZED LOCOMOTIVES BROUGHT IN AFTER NATIONALIZATION, STANDARD 'BRITANNIA' 4-6-2, 'MERCURY' STANDS AT PRESTON STATION WITH A PARCELS TRAIN IN NOVEMBER 1965.

■ THE SWANSEA TO SHREWSBURY TRAIN PASSES
THE SIGNAL BOX AT BUCKNALL, DRAWN BY A BR
STANDARD CLASS '5MT' 4-6-0.

CLASSIFICATIONS

British Railways used a modified version of the LMS classification system. Each locomotive class had a number from 0–9 that represented its power (0 for least powerful and 9 for most), with a suffix of F or P, or both (P first), to signify freight or passenger. Freight power ranged from 0–9, passenger from 0–8 but when freight and passenger classifications were equal, e.g. for the LMS Black Fives 5P5F, they became 5MT. 'Mixed traffic' locos had power in the range of classes 2–6.

Guard John Kerley remembered the gradual process of standardization:
British Rail had standardized brake vans by the mid 1950s and they were fitted with a periscope so the guard could see over the top. Guard's vans were always freezing though – until British standard vans came in you had a little cubby hole in the corner of the van with a tiny heater and a little coal fire that would get white hot sometimes, with the draught created by your speed. In the guard's van in the early days you also had a little cooker where you cooked your breakfast. I'd always managed a very nice fry up by the time we got to Peterborough! All that stopped with standardization!

■ THE COMBINED
POWERS OF TWO BR
STANDARD CLASS
LOCOMOTIVES WERE
NEEDED TO TAKE THE
'CAMBRIAN COAST
EXPRESS' TO THE
SUMMIT OF TALERDDIG
ON 9 JULY 1966.

Driver Bill Sidwell was sad at the disappearance of the big four regions but the standardization that followed nationalization had some benefits, as he recalled:

I was at Gloucester in 1948 when nationalization came and I can honestly say it made absolutely no difference to me, but on the dot – at midnight on the day it happened – all the trains in the area blew their whistles. I remember my phone ringing at around this time. The caller said that a train had been derailed on the Great Western. We were the London and Midland but we had a crane that would be suitable for this particular derailment. When the person on the other end of the line said he wanted the crane he said he wanted it for the British Railways Board – it sounded so strange because it was the first time I'd heard the name.

■ ALTHOUGH PERFECTLY ADEQUATE, THE NEW BRITISH RAILWAYS DINING CARS (ABOVE) LACKED THE CHARACTER OF THEIR ELEGANT PREDECESSORS.

■ WITH THE AID OF A REAR BANKER, BR 'CLAN' CLASS 4-6-2 NO. 72003 CLIMBS SHAP WITH A LIVERPOOL TO GLASGOW EXPRESS ON 5 AUGUST 1960.

Bill thinks nationalization was a good thing in many ways – it helped speed up the exchange of information and ideas between different areas, but financially it made little initial difference.
When nationalization took effect the railways were very run down – that was largely because of the war and the lack of funds that resulted from it. Before that the government had always taken the profits the railways had made, but they never put anything back. To some extent that situation continued when nationalization came. The move from steam to diesel was all done on a shoestring. Some railways even toyed with the idea of running buses – they had quite a fleet for taking stuff from various depots. Rail never went sufficiently in search of business because for so long – particularly during the war – they'd had a virtual monopoly on transport.

Nationalization also meant that, at last, standard locomotives began to be built and they were still being built as diesel trains began to come in. Edinburgh driver Sandy Begg had a less than enthusiastic view of at least one aspect of standardization:
By the time I'd started to drive full time, most of the engines were British Rail Standards, which no one liked – ironic really when you consider that they were supposed to combine the best features from all the old engines!

■ BR STANDARD 2-6-4T NO.80093 (ABOVE LEFT) SIMMERS ALONGSIDE THE TINY PLATFORM AT KILLIN WITH THE 09.56 TO KILLIN JUNCTION ON 4 AUGUST 1965.

■ BR STANDARD CLASS '9F' 2-10-0 No. 92073 (ABOVE) AWAITS ITS NEXT TURN OF DUTY AT WELLINGBOROUGH SHED ON 7 MAY 1965.

New Colours for a New Railway

Almost as soon as the big four railway companies became one in 1948 the race was on to find a new livery – a colour that would symbolize and unify the new and exciting world of British Railways.

Tom Shackle recalled those heady days:

I can remember that the new company presented its livery ideas at Olympia in Kensington, which was best known for its annual Ideal Home exhibition. It was all well and good to decide after a display like that, but I don't think they chose their colours wisely – I seem to recall that blue was chosen for passenger express engines but it only lasted a year or so, because no sooner had a cleaned engine started work than it looked absolutely filthy! The blue they chose just showed the dirt as badly as if it had been white – which showed how much the new management knew about railways! The choice of black for shunting engines was about the only sensible decision they made!

THE FIRST BR LOGO

In the late 1940s, the newly formed British Transport Commission devised a symbol for British Railways: a red wheel with a black panel across it carrying the white inscription 'British Railways', sat underneath a gold lion. Both right- and left-hand versions were produced so that the lion always faced forward, whichever side of the engine it was on.

- ADORNED WITH THE NEW GO-FASTER BR LOGO (LEFT), VALE OF RHEIDOL 2-6-2T No.8 'LLYWELYN' STANDS IN ABERYSTWYTH STATION WITH A TRAIN FOR DEVIL'S BRIDGE ON 2 JUNE 1977.

- SPORTING ITS NEW APPLE GREEN BRITISH RAILWAYS LIVERY (TOP), EX-LNER 'B17/4' CLASS 4-6-0 No.61665, 'LEICESTER CITY', IS SEEN AT LONDON, LIVERPOOL STREET IN SEPTEMBER 1948.

- EX-LMS CLASS '3P' 4-4-2T No.41975 (ABOVE) STANDS AT SEATON JUNCTION IN 1959.

Ken Williams remembered that there were still regional variations – Southern kept its green for example – but among the travelling public there was sadness at the disappearance of the old companies and their distinctive colours:

The Great Western Railway had beautiful colours and the new British Railways' efforts seemed poor in comparison. GWR locomotives were chrome green framed with red; the carriages were a lovely warm two-tone chocolate and cream colour. LNER used apple green on passenger locomotives but with gold lettering.

The joke was that the new railway executive was far keener on getting a unified look for the new company than sorting out its structural problems, but then I suppose paint was cheaper than rolling stock and manpower!

'The choice of black for shunting engines was about the only sensible decision they made!'

■ CLASS '2MT' 2-6-2T No.41221 STOPS AT THE PICTURESQUE HAMLET OF TORVER ON THE CONISTON BRANCH IN JULY 1951.

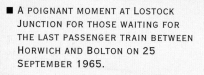

■ A POIGNANT MOMENT AT LOSTOCK
JUNCTION FOR THOSE WAITING FOR
THE LAST PASSENGER TRAIN BETWEEN
HORWICH AND BOLTON ON 25
SEPTEMBER 1965.

LAST DAY OF SERVICE

A long slow decline had meant that enthusiasts had plenty of time to prepare for the end of the steam era. Crowds gathered to see off the locomotives on their final day of service as trains 'steamed' off for the very last time.

- BR STANDARD CLASS '4MT' 2-6-4T No.80039 (LEFT) WAITS TO DEPART WITH THE LAST STEAM TRAIN FROM ILFRACOMBE ON 19 SEPTEMBER 1965.

- A SPECIAL TRAIN AT CLEOBURY MORTIMER (BELOW LEFT) ON 21 MAY 1955, PULLED BY EX-GREAT WESTERN RAILWAY DEAN GOODS 0-6-0 No. 2516.

- 30 APRIL 1967 WAS THE LAST DAY OF SERVICE ON THE CROMFORD & HIGH PEAK BRANCH IN DERBYSHIRE (BELOW). HERE, CLASS 'J94' 0-6-0STs No.68012 AND 68006 STORM UP HOPTON BANK WITH AN SLS SPECIAL.

- THE MUCH LOVED 'HAYLING BILLY' (FAR LEFT) LEAVES NORTH HAYLING ON ITS LAST DAY OF SERVICE ON THE HAVANT TO HAYLING ISLAND BRANCHLINE, 2 NOVEMBER 1963.

- AN ALCOHOLIC PRESENTATION IS MADE (LEFT) TO THE CREW OF CLASS '02' 0-4-4T No.14 'FISHBOURNE' AT WROXALL STATION ON THE LAST DAY OF STEAM SERVICES ON THE ISLE OF WIGHT, 17 APRIL 1966.

Beeching Cuts Deep

Before the infamous Beeching Cuts of the early 1960s, the railway system in Britain linked remote villages and hamlets as they had been linked back in the days when the motor car was still a fantasy of the future. But the old system was not profitable and as costs mounted the Conservative Government appointed Sir Richard Beeching (1913–85) to prune the unprofitable lines and turn the railways from a service into a business.

Despite his cuts, which began in 1963, the system never became profitable and what had been an unprofitable service was now neither a service nor profitable. Labour Transport Minister Barbara Castle tried to reverse many of the cuts on the grounds that remote rural lines were socially useful even if they could not pay their way, but by the time legislation was enacted in 1968 it was too late for many of the old lines.

Vinsun Gulliver, who was passed for driving in 1930, knew the pre-Beeching railway in Cheshire and the north west. He regretted the fact that the Beeching Cuts made the service less comprehensive, but wasn't entirely starry-eyed about the old days:

I drove the trains round Macclesfield and Liverpool, all local stuff, and all disappeared with the Beeching Cuts. It was strange to see them go – for years you could see the tracks stretching into the distance with the grass and weeds growing ever higher through them. Or the track was quickly dug up with just a few of the old station buildings turned into houses. But for us driving was just a job and we carried on driving elsewhere; we weren't romantic

■ IN HIS REPORT, ENTITLED 'THE RESHAPING OF BRITISH RAILWAYS', DR RICHARD BEECHING PROPOSED CLOSING 6,000 MILES OF UNECONOMIC RURAL AND CROSS-COUNTRY ROUTES, CLOSING 2,300 STATIONS AND SCRAPPING 9,000 STEAM LOCOMOTIVES. THE RED LINES ON THIS MAP SHOW THE LINES THAT WERE CLOSED DURING BEECHING'S CHAIRMANSHIP.

■ APPOINTED AS CHAIRMAN OF THE BRITISH RAILWAYS BOARD IN 1963, DR RICHARD BEECHING WAS THE MASTERMIND BEHIND THE WHOLESALE DESTRUCTION OF BRITAIN'S RAILWAYS. FOR HIS GOOD WORK HE WAS MADE A LIFE PEER IN 1965.

'... for years you could see the tracks stretching into the distance with the grass and weeds growing ever higher through them.'

about steam the way people were once steam vanished.

For passengers things were sadder and more inconvenient. In Norfolk, Betty Westall recalled:

In our village near Swaffham we saw the old trains going by and thought they'd always be there. Then suddenly they were gone – which was O.K. for those with cars, but I hated getting the bus into town to shop. One of the station buildings is still there at Great Dunham but any sign of the tracks has long vanished.

Harry Horn, who was born in Devon in 1904, started work on the Devon railway in 1919. Eighty years later, he was still working, but as a volunteer and on the same railway. Harry was lucky because the branchline on which he spent the last four decades of his official paid career just happened to be one that local enthusiasts were prepared to save.

Harry was lampboy at Starcross Station when horses were still used in the shunting yards. He recalls the wealth of full-time station staff:

A goods porter, a parcels porter, two junior porters and what they called a pier porter, who helped passengers getting off the trains

and on to the ferry that went between Starcross Station and Exmouth.

Harry trained as a signalman before moving into the station house at Stogumber in 1948.

High in the Quantocks, Stogumber is one of the prettiest stations in England and it is the station at which Harry was still working long after the Beeching Cuts. The Minehead-Taunton line was the only branchline left in the West Country after Beeching, but in 1971 it too finally closed. By this time Harry and his wife had bought their house so they stayed put and watched the railway slowly become overgrown and derelict. But the old railway buildings and track were not destroyed and some time later local enthusiasts re-started a steam service, which continues today – a rare case of survival against all the odds.

■ ONE OF THE FAMOUS STANIER EX-LMS 'BLACK FIVE' 4-6-0S (RIGHT) BEING BROKEN UP AT COHEN'S SCRAPYARD IN THE MID 1960S.

'I don't think he was really brought in to make the railways more rational and profitable'

■ FEBRUARY 28, 1959 WAS A SAD DAY IN RAILWAY HISTORY AS IT HERALDED THE END OF THE MIDLAND & GREAT NORTHERN JOINT RAILWAY SYSTEM. HERE, ON THE LAST DAY, IVATT 2-6-0 No.43161, ALLOCATED TO 32F YARMOUTH BEACH, IS SEEN APPROACHING WESTON WITH THE 09.02 TRAIN FROM YARMOUTH. THE LOCOMOTIVE CARRIES A SCRIBBLED HEADBOARD READING 'THAT'S YER LOT', WHICH HAD, APPARENTLY, BEEN ATTACHED BY LOCAL DRIVERS AS AN IRREVERENT BUT PITHY EPITAPH.

BEWARE OF TRAINS.

MID & G.N.
JOINT RAILWAY.
—NOTICE—
TRESPASSERS
WILL BE PROSECUTED

■ DRAUGHTON
CROSSING DURING
THE DISMANTLING OF
THE CLOSED MARKET
HARBOROUGH TO
NORTHAMPTON LINE.

Lowestoft stationmaster Rod Lock, who started work in the 1940s, could see the sense in some Beeching Cuts but not all:

East Winch survived the 1963 cuts but disappeared in 1968 when the second major cuts were made. The King's Lynn to Norwich line also went then and I think that was very silly. East Winch, a tiny out-of-the-way station maybe, but Norfolk to Kings Lynn was a busy route.

Under-use was the real problem, not waste or inefficiency, as Rod recalled:

There was enormous attention to detail; if a station was £1 short in its accounting there would be a full investigation.

Tom Shackle saw the Beeching Cuts as just another mistake in a long line of mistakes:

Well, I don't think he was really brought in to make the railways more rational and profitable. He was simply brought in to cut the losses the government was making – he could have recommended more investment, which in the long run might have attracted more passengers and made the railways pay in that way. Instead he saved money but made what remained of the railways even less attractive. After years of failing to invest the government just made blunder after blunder and the Beeching blunder was the biggest of the lot.

■ A STANIER 8F 2-8-0
LIES ABANDONED IN
THE CLOSED DEPOT
YARD AT TRAFFORD
PARK, MANCHESTER IN
THE 1960S.

NEW USES FOR OLD LINES

The dismantling of hundreds of miles of track after the Beeching cuts left empty cuttings, embankments and tunnels and long stretches of grassy roads to nowhere. Gradually the routes have been reclaimed for other purposes, most commonly walks, cycling routes and pleasure trails.

■ SEEN HERE AT TORSIDE (RIGHT), THE LONGDENDALE TRAIL USES THE TRACKBED OF THE FORMER SHEFFIELD TO MANCHESTER LINE BETWEEN HADFIELD AND WOODHEAD.

■ ELECTRICITY PYLONS FOLLOWING THE PATH OF THE FORMER TRANS-PENNINE ROUTE BETWEEN SHEFFIELD AND MANCHESTER (LEFT & BELOW) AND MAKING USE OF THE WOODHEAD TUNNEL TO ROUTE THE CABLES THROUGH THE HILLSIDE.

■ HIDDEN AWAY IN A REMOTE VALLEY IN THE SCENIC PEAK DISTRICT, THE LEEK & MANIFOLD VALLEY LIGHT RAILWAY (ABOVE) HAD A VERY SHORT LIFE OF ONLY 30 YEARS. FOLLOWING CLOSURE IN 1934, THE TRACKBED WAS GIVEN BY ITS OWNERS, THE LONDON MIDLAND & SCOTTISH RAILWAY, TO STAFFORDSHIRE COUNTY COUNCIL TO USE AS A FOOTPATH AND CYCLEWAY.

■ NORTHEAST OF OBAN, CONNELL BRIDGE (RIGHT) WAS ORIGINALLY CONSTRUCTED TO CARRY ONLY RAIL TRAFFIC. IT WAS CONVERTED IN 1914 TO TAKE BOTH CARS AND TRAINS BUT SINCE THE CLOSURE OF THE BALLACHULISH BRANCH LINE IN 1966 HAS ONLY CARRIED ROAD TRAFFIC.

'It was all left to committees to decide the fate of the rail system and of course committees always lead to disaster'

Decline and Fall – The Failure to Invest

The railways were vital to the war effort yet during and after the war successive governments hived off railway profits that should have gone back into the system. The results were hugely damaging and created a legacy from which we have still not fully recovered.

Tom Shackle recalled the creation of British Railways in 1948:
It was a right muddle after the initial period when absolutely nothing seemed to have happened! Mind you, it must have been difficult to turn four very different and very competitive railway companies into one. The railways had no responsible minister either – it was all left to committees to decide the fate of the rail system and of course committees always lead to disaster.

■ IN THE LAST MONTHS OF STEAM OPERATION ON THE ISLE OF WIGHT CLASS 'O2' 0-4-4T NO.14 'FISHBOURNE' RECEIVES ATTENTION AT RYDE ST JOHN'S ENGINE SHED.

■ A BEDRAGGLED-LOOKING BR 'BRITTANIA' CLASS 4-6-2 NO.70014, 'IRON DUKE' STRUGGLES UP SHAP NEAR SCOUT GREEN ON ITS WAY TO GLASGOW IN JULY 1967.

■ WITH THE INEXORABLE RUNDOWN OF STEAM RAILWAYS ALREADY IN PROCESS, NOT EVERY LOCOMOTIVE WAS GIVEN THE SKILLED ATTENTION IT REQUIRED TO KEEP IT IN THE BEST CONDITION. INEVITABLY, THIS AFFECTED ENGINES' ABILITY TO COPE WITH DEMANDING TERRAIN OR CHALLENGING CONDITIONS. HERE, EX-GWR 2-8-0 NO.3850 STRUGGLES WITH THE FREEZING WEATHER OF THE WINTER OF 1962/3 (BELOW).

I can remember stations that had not been touched since the 1930s and even the 1920s – paint coming off rusty wagons in the yards, piles of old broken equipment, and even the signs telling you the name of the station were almost illegible in some cases. I'm sure the government would have said that there was no money for repairs and restoration – the country was nearly bankrupt it is true, but it was short-sighted so badly to neglect our most important transport system.

There were definitely more accidents too as the network became more rundown – a terrible crash in 1952 and another in 1957 killed something like 200 people. The situation was similar to the Ladbroke Grove crash that followed the more recent privatization – when you put maintenance out to tender and take the cheapest bid you have no control over the company doing the work and they will always cut corners. In the late 1940s and early 1950s they didn't just cut corners – they let things fall apart.

I remember we'd had a car in the 1930s and like other well-off people we tried our best to avoid the trains – even then when the system wasn't too bad – but by the 1950s you avoided those dirty shabby stations like the plague, so eventually the train became synonymous with a bad experience. It wasn't the same on the Continent, where huge amounts were invested in the railway before and especially after the war, and the result is that today train travel is better and cheaper almost anywhere on the Continent than it is here!

By the end of the war you have to remember that we were still using thousands of locomotives that had been built at the turn of the century nearly 50 years earlier and many carriages looked like something from a museum. I remember often travelling in carriages that had been built while Victoria was still on the throne – you could still just about see all their fine woodwork, delicate wrought-iron brackets and wonderful wood panelling, but it had all gone to seed. It was all very sad.

Ken Williams recalled the days of the railway in the late 1950s and early 1960s as continued lack of investment led to closures, cutbacks, shabby engines and unkempt stations – and ultimately, of course, to the Beeching Cuts:

The big problem was that the country had never really recovered from the war. Germany and Japan had to be rebuilt with American money but the UK was allowed to just flounder on as best it could – it really is hard now to recall how badly off we all were. Only a very few very rich people could afford foreign holidays, for example. The railways suffered badly from the lack of money, I think, and from the fact that people were beginning to switch to cars in a big way – you'd do anything to be able to buy a car and the old glamour of the railways had gone. You could see the results of the lack of money everywhere – paint peeling on local stations and even on the big glamorous London stations; engines not running as well as they might because they were being badly cleaned and repaired; and carriages had a tired and worn look.

But for the railway enthusiast it could be exciting – we saw ancient stock still at work and the yards still full of horses and old railway carts that were still being used. I believe some of these were still being used in the 1960s.

■ ONE OF THE MANY NON-STANDARD CLASSES OF LOCOMOTIVE THAT BRITISH RAILWAYS INHERITED WERE THESE ANCIENT LONDON & SOUTH WESTERN RAILWAY'S DRUMMOND CLASS 'T9' 4-4-0S. HERE No.30120, BUILT IN 1899 AND THE ONLY ONE OF ITS CLASS PRESERVED IN LATER YEARS, SPENDS ITS LAST DAYS ON LIGHT PASSENGER DUTIES IN NORTH CORNWALL.

■ LEAKING STEAM, WORN OUT CLASS '02' 0-4-4T No.35 'FRESHWATER' LEAVES WROXALL, ISLE OF WIGHT, WITH A RYDE TO VENTNOR TRAIN ON 1 SEPTEMBER 1965.

Denys Watkins Pitchford remembered how the gloom of wartime travelling lingered long after the war was over and how rail travel revealed that the country really was broke:

This was the era during which rail travel changed from being something people loved to being a much more practical thing – if you had to go to work or to see relatives you went by train if you didn't have a car, but a lot of the pleasure had gone. The interiors of the carriages in the early 1950s looked like they hadn't been touched in decades – and they looked like that because they really hadn't been touched. There were broken light fittings, bare bulbs, dirty windows that no longer fitted properly and warped wooden panels and window frames. It was enjoyable in a way to be in a carriage probably made just after the Great War – I can remember being in such a carriage myself – because it was a beautifully made and atmospheric thing, but we wanted to escape the dark gloomy wartime feeling that persisted well into the 1950s. We wanted things to be bright and new, we wanted technology, clean lines and an end to shabbiness. Shabbiness is what train journeys were about then and we didn't want it.

■ ALTHOUGH ONLY ABOUT 20 YEARS OLD, EX-LNER CLASS 'B1' 4-6-0 No.61404 LOOKS DECIDEDLY NEGLECTED AS IT NEARS THE END OF ITS DAYS WORKING A THORNTON JUNCTION TO CRAIL TRAIN IN AUGUST 1961.

THE BREAKER'S YARD

Despite the deep affection in which steam locomotives were held by the general public, there wasn't much that could be done with them, once they'd been taken out of service. A handful were saved by enthusiasts and steam preservation groups but hundreds of locomotives were left to rust and decay in breaker's yards.

■ A SAD SCENE AT COHEN'S CRANSLEY SCRAPYARD NEAR KETTERING WHERE A WIDE VARIETY OF STEAM LOCOMOTIVES WERE BROKEN UP DURING THE 1960S. MANY OF TODAY'S PRESERVED STEAM LOCOMOTIVES WERE RESCUED FROM THE SCRAPYARD AND CAN ONCE AGAIN BE SEEN OPERATING ON ROUTES AROUND BRITAIN; ALTHOUGH THESE WERE NOT SO LUCKY.

■ DESPITE HAVING LOST ITS CHIMNEY, THIS WITHDRAWN 'JUBILEE' CLASS 4-6-0 (BELOW LEFT) STILL RETAINS ITS NAMEPLATE — WHAT MUST IT BE WORTH NOW?

■ THE END OF STEAM ON THE SOUTHERN REGION HERALDED BRITAIN'S LAST REGULAR EXPRESS PASSENGER STEAM OPERATIONS. FOLLOWING THE END OF STEAM IN 1967, BR STANDARD CLASS '5MT' NO.73093 AWAITS DISPOSAL AT WEYMOUTH ENGINE SHED.

■ LONG LINES OF WITHDRAWN STEAM LOCOMOTIVES AWAIT THE BREAKER'S TORCH AT SWINDON.

■ A GRAFFITI ARTIST WITH A MACABRE SENSE OF HUMOUR (FAR LEFT) PUTS A LESS THAN A BRAVE FACE ON A CONDEMNED LOCOMOTIVE AT WOODHAMS YARD, BARRY DOCKS, GLAMORGAN, 1968

■ FORMER GWR LOCOMOTIVES 0-4-2T NO.1435 AND 'KING' CLASS 4-6-0 NO. 6013 'KING HENRY VIII' FORLORNLY AWAIT DISPOSAL AT SWINDON WORKS IN OCTOBER 1962.

THE RAILWAYMEN –
ON THE TRAINS

Their jobs were demanding and often exhausting, but the men employed on steam trains showed a dedication and pride in their work that would seem rare nowadays.

Drivers

Drivers were the heroes of the old railway – they were one step down from God, as one old railwayman remembered! They were idolized by generations of schoolchildren who aspired to the footplate and a life in charge of one of the wonders of the Industrial Revolution.

The drivers were a proud lot too, as Reg Coote, driver on the Southern Railway, recalled:

In the drivers' lobby or common room the Chatham men would sit at one end with the Brighton blokes at the other and they'd never talk to each other. And men in different areas tried to keep themselves apart from everyone else – the drivers at Nine Elms, for example, always wore bow ties. It was a way of saying who they were and if, of course, they met another man with a dicky bow they knew instantly they were mates. This is probably why the men at each different depot had group nicknames too – like the Dover Sharks or the Old Kent Roaders!

■ PREVIOUS PAGE: THE DRIVER OF LMS 0-6-2 TANK LOCOMOTIVE No.6926 WAITS PATIENTLY FOR THE SIGNAL TO MOVE. ORIGINALLY DESIGNED BY FRANCIS WEBB (1836–1906) FOR THE LONDON & NORTH WESTERN RAILWAY IN 1898, MANY OF THESE WORKHORSES SURVIVED UNTIL THE 1950S.

■ ALTHOUGH OPEN TO ALL WEATHERS, BOTH DRIVER AND FIREMAN SEEM TO BE VERY RELAXED ON THE SPOTLESS FOOTPLATE OF THIS LONDON & NORTH WESTERN RAILWAY LOCOMOTIVE AT CHESTER.

Drivers were sticklers for tradition. Near Gillingham in Kent, an old driver Reg had known, called Dizzy Farrow, was buried, and for years after he died every driver coming along the track by the graveyard would toot Dizzy as he went by.

For drivers, canteens or common rooms were as strictly demarcated as the passenger waiting rooms, as Reg recalled:

Cleaners at Stewarts Lane, as elsewhere, had their own lobby – a sort of common room – and in those days it was completely separate from the drivers' and firemen's lobby. We all ate separately and once you were a fireman or driver you never went in the cleaners' room and they never came in ours.

In the drivers' lobby the windows were covered with tar during the war because of the blackout and there was always a huge open fire, a long table with a two-inch-thick top and a wooden form – a bit like a school bench – bolted to the floor just in case you might walk out with it under your arm! That's where we all ate whatever food we had.

■ THE DRIVER OF EX-GWR 2-8-0 No.3804 DAMPS DOWN THE COAL AS HE WAITS FOR THE ROAD ON THE DOCKS BRANCH AT OVER JUNCTION, GLOUCESTER ON 15 NOVEMBER 1962.

■ BIRD'S EYE VIEW OF THE FOOTPLATE CREW OF THIS EX-GREAT WESTERN RAILWAY LOCOMOTIVE, BELIEVED TO BE A 43XX CLASS 2-6-0, NEAR OXFORD, C1965.

'I could keep my eyes closed and always tell by the noise of the engine where we were'

■ IN MARCH 1968
THE DRIVER OF THIS
LOCOMOTIVE FACES AN
UNCERTAIN FUTURE –
THERE ARE ONLY JUST
OVER FOUR MONTHS
TO GO BEFORE THE
END OF STEAM ON
BRITISH RAILWAYS.

When diesels came in, many of the older drivers never got the hang of the new engines but, as Scottish driver Sandy Begg remembered, that wasn't always the case:

Many of us, myself included, went to school to learn how to drive the diesels and most of the old drivers became good diesel men, but those early diesels were always breaking down, unlike the older steam engines, which were incredibly reliable.

David Lubbock, who started work as a cleaner in 1945, remembered the unique skills of the driver:

I was now in the old MGN region, which we always called the Muddle and Get Nowhere Railway, but working at Parkeston near Harwich we were dealing with troop trains a lot of the time and they were run in a far more sophisticated way. When I was driving, the thing I remember most was the noise. I could keep my eyes closed and always tell by the noise of the engine where we were. I never got it wrong, that's how well I knew the road. But like most of the drivers I didn't have a watch – didn't need one. Keeping time was all a matter of experience.

176 *Memories of Steam*

That sense that drivers learned best by learning on the job disappeared with the coming of electric and diesel, and drivers went off to school, at least partly, to learn how to do it, an idea that horrified Billy Westall:

The old boys I remember who learned to drive before the Great War would have laughed at that. Most of them couldn't read or write much anyway, but they were brilliant on the footplate and could do their work blindfold.

Scottish driver Jim McClelland recalled the way in which drivers coped with responsibility and how they gained experience:

All drivers were given a route card and asked to sign it – and woe betide you if you signed to say you knew the route and then there was an accident and it transpired that you didn't really know the route well enough. In practice that never actually happened because no one would be mad enough to say they knew a route when they didn't. If there was the least mishap there would be an enquiry and that card would be evidence.

■ PASSENGERS HAVE ALWAYS BEEN FASCINATED BY STEAM ENGINES, ESPECIALLY NEW LOCOMOTIVES. HERE, ONE POSES WITH THE PROUD CREW OF A NEWLY DELIVERED LMS FAIRBURN 2-6-4T NO.2277, c1947.

'Most of them couldn't read or write much anyway, but they were brilliant on the footplate and could do their work blindfold'

■ ONE OF THE LAST STEAM TURNS ON BRITISH RAILWAYS, LOSTOCK HALL 'BLACK FIVE' 4-6-0 NO.45407 RECEIVES ATTENTION FROM ITS DRIVER AT GARSTANG BEFORE RETURNING TO PRESTON ON 26 JULY 1968.

■ THE CAB OF EX-GWR PUSH-PULL 0-4-2T NO.1451 AT GLOUCESTER IN FEBRUARY 1964.

In other respects the system used peer pressure to make sure the men were kept up to the mark. Drivers didn't want their firemen to fail as drivers, for example, because failure was a reflection on *them*. To prevent this sort of problem arising they made sure the fireman had enough experience to get him through. Jim again:

Drivers would let you have a go when you were a fireman. I had a go at driving while I was still a fireman, but I was always under the supervision of an experienced man so it was always safe. To get ahead quickly it was also a good idea to sign up for a number of routes – that way you got a lot more driving turns and, eventually, when you'd done enough turns, more money.

Jim also remembered the rigorous testing of would-be drivers and some of the sadnesses involved with the transition from steam to diesel:

The boss would test you on all the rules and regulations and he was always very thorough. He took you on the footplate, asked you all about the layout, how the vacuum brake worked, how one should react in an emergency – it was all very rigorous.

■ Ex-LMS 'Jubilee'
Class 4-6-0
No.45675 'Hardy'
stops for water at
Keighley on 23 June
1966.

And it was the inspectors who had to pass the old steam drivers on the new diesel trains, as Jim explains:
Some of the older men were terrible when it came to learning to drive diesel – you could see the look of despair on their faces. Their lives had been so tied up with steam that they could make nothing of this new-fangled system. Some adapted but many left. And it didn't matter that the new cabs were cleaner and more comfortable than the old footplate. It didn't matter that a steam train driver's work was very dirty work indeed. They loved it and they missed it.

Vinsun Gulliver, who was driving as far back as the 1920s, always remembered the strictness and self-discipline of the drivers:
If you met the drivers I knew as a young man today you'd say they were a hard unfeeling lot. They were hard certainly – and hard-drinking in my recollection – but driving was a hard life then in all weathers and you were paid a pittance. There were the shifts too and long years ahead before you could hope for a half-decent pension. Worst of all I remember driving in terrible weather – impossible to describe how awful that could be, hour after hour on the footplate.

EXTREME WEATHER

Conditions in open cabs could be uncomfortable at the best of times, but freezing weather, floods and snow could test drivers and maintenance crew to the limit to keep trains moving.

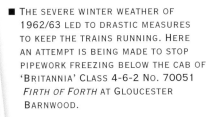

■ THE SEVERE WINTER WEATHER OF 1962/63 LED TO DRASTIC MEASURES TO KEEP THE TRAINS RUNNING. HERE AN ATTEMPT IS BEING MADE TO STOP PIPEWORK FREEZING BELOW THE CAB OF 'BRITANNIA' CLASS 4-6-2 NO. 70051 *FIRTH OF FORTH* AT GLOUCESTER BARNWOOD.

■ BANKED IN THE REAR BY A 2-6-2 TANK, A HEAVY COAL TRAIN FROM SOUTH WALES STRUGGLES UP SAPPERTON BANK (BELOW LEFT) IN THE FREEZING CONDITIONS OF JANUARY 1963 BEFORE DISAPPEARING INTO THE MURKY DEPTHS OF SAPPERTON TUNNEL (BELOW RIGHT).

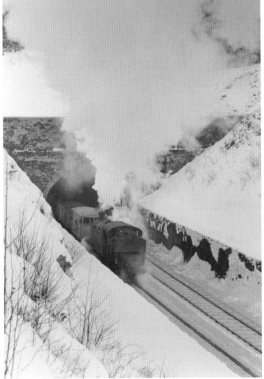

■ A MIXED FREIGHT HAULED BY A WESTERN REGION 'HALL' CLASS 4-6-0 STORMS THROUGH THE COTSWOLDS NEAR FRAMPTON MANSELL DURING THE SEVERE WEATHER OF JANUARY 1963.

■ SEVERE FLOODING IN THE CULM VALLEY IN DEVON DURING OCTOBER 1960 DIDN'T STOP THE PASSAGE OF THIS TRAIN THROUGH HELE & BRADNINCH (FAR LEFT) AND SILVERTON (LEFT).

181

Firemen

In the days of steam the driver had the glamorous job but the really hard work on the footplate was done by the fireman.

Dick Potts, who started work in Birmingham in 1949, recalled:

It took me about a week to get the hang of firing, but at Bordsley it was all firing on shunting engines – the first step for a fireman. It was hard work because it was very busy – it was a shed that worked 24 hours a day, seven days a week.

When you were firing on a shunting engine you needed plenty of steam, particularly where you were moving wagons full of heavy freight like coal. But you didn't want too much power – too much meant sparks in the chimney and wasted heat. And all the time he was keeping the fire going the fireman had to watch the boiler and keep the cab clean – drivers could be fussy buggers!

I still maintain that firing was more interesting than driving. It took a great deal of skill to do well because a lot of the time you had to adapt your firing technique to the particular driver. If he was a bit heavy-handed you'd need more fire. But too much fire with a good driver would be a disaster. Or you might get an engine from another area – a foreign engine as we used to say – and you might never really work out how to fire it.

■ THE FIREMAN HAS A BRIEF OPPORTUNITY FOR A CONVERSATION AT THE ENGINE AWAITS THE SIGNAL FOR DEPARTURE FROM WROXALL ON THE ISLE OF WIGHT., 30 AUGUST 1965.

Jim McClelland, who worked for the LMS for almost 50 years, remembered how firemen were trained:
When I started, cleaners were not allowed any firing turns on mainline trains till they were 17, but they were allowed to fire on branchlines. The first engine on which I fired – No. 17375 – was ancient. You had to be careful with the water pressure, because if it got too high and there was a blow-off you then found you couldn't get the injector on. It was just a peculiarity of that old engine.

A good fireman was aware that every locomotive has its own individual characteristics. Some locomotives had sloping fireboxes, others had long fireboxes; the Duchess class had a very wide firebox and it was always the devil to fire it from cold. I remember working as a fireman with drivers who would never talk to you when the train was going in one direction but would chat quite happily if it was going in the other direction!

■ THE FIREMAN OF CLASS 'A1X' 0-6-0T No.32650 PREPARES TO SWITCH THE POINTS FOR THE LOCO TO RUN ROUND ITS TRAIN ON THE LAST DAY OF SERVICE AT HAYLING ISLAND STATION, 2 NOVEMBER 1963.

■ A HOT AND GRIMY JOB — A STEAM RAISER AT BOURNEMOUTH ENGINE SHED DURING THE LAST DAYS OF STEAM ON THE SOUTHERN REGION IN THE SUMMER OF 1967.

The Railwaymen – on the Trains **183**

'...firing was more interesting than driving – it took a great deal of skill to do well'

■ DRIVER AND FIREMAN ON THE FOOTPLATE OF SOUTHERN RAILWAY 'N' CLASS 2-6-0 NO.1407, BUILT AT ASHFORD WORKS IN 1933.

■ SHOVELLING CHAR FROM THE SMOKEBOX OF AN EX-NORTH EASTERN RAILWAY 'Q6' CLASS 0-8-0 AT WEST HARTLEPOOL SHED.

Allan Richardson, a third-generation driver on the LNER, had similar memories: he reckoned a fireman would shift 45lb of coal per mile on average. But happiness was all down to a good shovel:

I used to hide mine every night under the breakdown train. A fireman's shovel has its own special design and they varied from region to region. They used to say it took four men even to lift a Great Western shovel! But generally speaking shunting shovels were short handled while shovels used on the big mainline engines had long handles, so you could get the coal well into the corners of the firebox. This was particularly important on the Pacifics because most of the coal was burned in the corners. We used to say that the best fireman kept the coal dancing on the firebars.

David Lubbock, who worked in East Anglia and started as a cleaner in the engine sheds in 1945, remembered the sheer effort involved:

Firing was very tiring till you got used to it. On some engines you were shovelling almost continually but on others you'd get plenty of time to pause between bouts of activity. A lot of it had to do with the driver too – with a really good driver you had less firing to do because you used less coal. With a poor driver you'd get through several lorry loads!

Fred Simpson, born in 1930, remembered firing on the Great Western in World War II:

A lot of men joined the railway to avoid being called up, but when they started firing they quickly decided the life wasn't for them – the work was far too hard!

Arthur Archer recalled the attitude of the footplate staff to their engines:

Some drivers and firemen loved their engines and treated them very carefully. They'd coax them along and make delicate adjustments to the controls to allow for changes in the road – either uphill or downhill – but some drivers were completely the opposite. Even the best built engine – and some were superbly built – wouldn't satisfy them. They would have thrashed everything from the worst engine to the best – it was just in them to be impatient.

■ THE JOB OF A LOCOMOTIVE FIREMAN WAS CRUCIAL TO THE EFFICIENT RUNNING OF THE LOCOMOTIVE AND MANY TOP LINK DRIVERS HAD THEIR FAVOURITE FIREMEN WITH WHOM THEY WORKED AS A TEAM. HERE THE FIREMAN CAREFULLY POSITIONS A CHARGE OF COAL INTO THE FIREBOX OF A 2-6-0.

MEMORIAL IN SOHAM CHURCH, CAMBRIDGESHIRE:

This tablet commemorates the heroic action of fireman J. W. Nightfall, G. C. who lost his life, & driver B. Gimbert, G. C. who was badly injured whilst detaching a blazing wagon from an ammunition train at Soham Station at 1.43am on June 2nd 1944. The station was totally destroyed and considerable damage done by the explosion. The devotion to duty of these brave men saved the town of Soham from grave destruction. Signalman F. Bridges was killed whilst on duty & guard H. Clarke suffered from shock,

'Be strong and quit yourselves like men' (1944)

■ WOMEN WERE ALSO EMPLOYED ON THE RAILWAYS DURING WORLD WAR I. HERE THE STATION STAFF AT TORPHINS IN SCOTLAND POSE FOR THE CAMERA.

■ ON THE BACKWELL COLLIERY SYSTEM IN THE 1960S (BELOW LEFT) THESE WORKERS' CLOTHES ARE HARDLY RECOGNISABLE AS UNIFORMS AT ALL.

■ STATION STAFF POSE FOR THE CAMERA (BELOW) AT INSTOW ON THE LONDON & SOUTH WESTERN RAILWAY'S BRANCH FROM BARNSTAPLE JUNCTION TO TORRINGTON, DURING THE LATE VICTORIAN ERA. THE SMART PLATFORM STAFF ARE IN STARK CONTRAST TO THE ROUGHLY DRESSED WORKMAN WHO KEEPS HIS PLACE ON THE TRACKBED.

BOOKING OFFICE.

DRESSED FOR THE JOB

Working with steam was a dirty job and the drivers, firemen and maintenance staff's clothes reflected this. Elsewhere on the network staff were expected to present themselves smartly. Their uniforms reflected the discipline and prestige associated with the job.

■ THE SMART BRITISH RAILWAYS UNIFORM OF 1964 IS SHOWN OFF IN THIS PUBLICITY PHOTOGRAPH.

■ AN EARLY TWENTIETH CENTURY LONDON & NORTH WESTERN RAILWAY GUARD FULLY KITTED OUT IN ILL-FITTING JACKET, WHISTLE AND GREEN FLAG.

■ DRIVERS WERE GLAMOROUS AND HIGHLY RESPECTED FIGURES, BUT THEIRS WAS A DIRTY JOB AND RUGGED OVERALLS THE APPROPRIATE OUTFIT FOR IT.

187

Guards

Now that the old-style guards have vanished from the scene it is hard to imagine the days when the guard was vital to the safety of train passengers.

John Kerley, who started guard training just after World War II, recalled how he learned the ropes: *I spent my first four weeks at King's Cross working closely with an experienced guard to get used to the various duties and routines. I'd start at 8am by reporting to the guard superintendent, who'd tell me which guard to report to. Then I'd be shown the sidings, because guards guarded the train as well as the passengers. We were responsible for backing trains into sidings – they were never driven in; always backed in with the guard directing operations and signalling to the driver who, of course, couldn't really see where he was going. It could be tricky, too, reversing into the sidings because you had to know all the signals and set backs.*

■ GREAT WESTERN RAILWAY PASSENGER GUARD (BELOW) GIVING THE SIGNAL FOR THE TRAIN TO DEPART, 1907.

■ A POSSIBLE DIFFERENCE OF OPINION BETWEEN THE GUARD AND CREW AT CHALFORD (ABOVE), ON 12 SEPTEMBER 1964.

There were no phones in those days, which meant that you had to use hand signals and lamps to get the driver to do what you wanted him to do. After four weeks I was put in front of the signals inspector who quizzed me on all the rules and regulations and working practices. I found it all a bit of an ordeal – inspectors in those days seemed solemn and terrifyingly important but I think I passed all right simply because I'd had a really good teacher. The guards in those days really knew their stuff. The other curious thing about this time was that you decided yourself when you were ready to go in front of the inspector. Might sound a funny way to do it but it actually worked very well because it put the onus on you to learn fast.

Nat Budgen remembered his days as a guard in the 1930s:

In these early days I worked mostly on what was called the empty coach link – that was the shift of men who brought empty coaches into London or took them out from London to Barnet and Enfield and the sidings. When we put the coaches together we had to check all the electrical connections to make sure all the lighting and so on would work, as well as the vacuum and steam pipes. We'd also check windows were closed and handbrakes off.

As guards working in the shunting yards we were so busy we hardly had time to breathe and though it was mucky work we were never given overalls, which always struck me as odd – firemen, cleaners and drivers all got overalls, but not us. Just one of the peculiarities of the old railway, I suppose.

'As guards working in the shunting yards we were so busy we hardly had time to breathe'

■ WAITING FOR THE SIGNAL, THE FOOTPLATE CREW OF EX-GREAT WESTERN RAILWAY 'KING' CLASS 4-6-0 NO.6005, 'KING GEORGE II', C1949.

But John Kerley was keen to emphasize that drivers relied heavily on the skill and experience of the guard:

If the main-line guard knew which of us had checked his train and put it together he'd know whether or not to make his own checks. In my day the guard was an important man – vital to the safe operation of the train. There were three links among the guards – the lowest, where we all started, was the empty coach link: you were simply getting coaches ready and bringing them to where they needed to be. Then – strictly according to seniority – you moved up to the local link; that meant you worked on trains doing local runs; the top link meant you were on main-line trains. There were also two volunteer links. These were for the Newcastle and Edinburgh run – they were volunteer routes because you had to lodge away from home, but they paid extra.

But guards were also given huge responsibility, as John Kerley remembered:

We used to make our own road books – these were notebooks where we drew the various routes and lines we needed to know, the position of signals and crossings on them.

There were always moments of drama, too – I remember trains occasionally lost steam on a steep incline north of Wood Green in north London, where what we called a jack catch was installed. This was a device designed to de-rail a train that lost all steam and began to slip back. We used N2 steam engines for local work and on another incline, this time towards Finsbury Park, they'd get stuck occasionally if they hadn't had a run at the hill or if the sand was poor and the line wet.

If the train stopped here we used to leap out and put detonators on the track – the idea was that when a relief train approached to give us a hand it would know how close it was to the stalled engine as it backed into position. The rescue engine driver would then blow what we called a cock crow on his whistle before he got going, with the stalled train behind him. I'd usually be out there with a lamp helping when this sort of thing happened – I remember, too, it was awful if you had to do all this in a tunnel because the noise of the detonators going off used to bring down great falls of soot from the tunnel roof. By the time you got out you were covered in the stuff. The drivers hated the noise of the detonators going off in tunnels, too, and they'd try to get you to put down fewer than you were supposed to.

■ AN LMS EXPRESS ABOUT TO DEPART FROM PLATFORM 15 AT EUSTON STATION IN 1938. THE GUARD IS RECEIVING THE 'RIGHT AWAY' SIGNAL FROM A COLLEAGUE WHILE THE STATION MASTER, DRESSED IN TOP HAT AND TAILS, LOOKS ON.

As time went by John found that he could spot problems long before they arose, although that didn't always mean he was able to do anything about them:

At Wood Green I could always tell when a train was about to get stuck – we'd have a run at the hill and if the engine and first carriage got over the top of the hill I knew we were all right. If the engine alone got over we were in trouble.

WILFRED OWEN

'Just put up here. Train was wickedly late. I travelled in the Guard's van. Sitting in the Guard's Nook I narrowly escaped being smashed by a passing goods' train. Some loose timber hit the coach just above my head. It awoke me with a big shock. This caused our train to stop a long while: I believe in order to telephone about the dangerous goods' train.'

Wilfred Owen, in a letter to his mother, Susan Owen (29 December 1916)

'The drivers hated the noise of the detonators going off in the tunnels'

In a situation like this the train stopping would mean delay and serious disruption to the timetable. *Drivers, guards and everyone else involved were proud of their good time-keeping – which is probably why we didn't get stuck that often. When it did happen I'd walk back to the nearest signal box so the signalman knew we'd blocked the line up ahead. The guard always had a vacuum brake in his van and that went down, too, if the train was stuck.*

When you think that the old Pullman train might weigh 440 tons you can see that they took some pulling and that there were bound to be problems now and then. The sand would always be running as we approached a hill (to help the wheels grip), but wet leaves, for example, were not such a problem in the steam days as they are now. The reason was that the old engines, which were very heavy, would crush through the leaves. Diesels are lighter and don't crush through, so they are more likely to slip. Snow was always more of a problem with diesel electrics too – it used to make their motors short out, something that obviously could never happen with steam trains. The only problem with snow in the steam era was that it mucked up the mechanical signalling.

I remember on the 7.45am to Leeds once there was so much snow that we didn't get back till three o'clock the following morning. That was caused by 2ft of snow and with that much snow all the signals broke down and you had to crawl along. You had to stop at every light and go back and protect your train with detonators under what was called time interval service – as a result of all this, journeys would be badly delayed.

With electronic signalling unaffected by weather, the responsibilities of all railway workers – but especially guards and porters – have been greatly reduced and that, of course, means that the jobs are more mundane, less satisfying than they were.

John also points out that guards and drivers were pretty close because they relied on each other. *They trusted each other because they had to.*

PICKING UP MAIL BAGS AT FULL SPEED

■ 192 BL [S&S 10442334] LETTERS BEING SORTED IN A GREAT WESTERN RAILWAY TRAVELLING POST OFFICE IN 1935.

■ AN OBVIOUSLY HAND-TOUCHED POSTCARD SHOWING A LONDON & NORTH WESTERN RAILWAY TRAVELLING POST OFFICE COLLECTING A BAG OF MAIL WHILE AT SPEED.

■ THIS CLUTTERED SCENE AT WIGAN ON 6 DECEMBER 1967 CLEARLY ILLUSTRATES JUST HOW MUCH MATERIAL USED TO BE TRANSPORTED BY RAIL IN THOSE DAYS.

MAIL TRAINS

Once upon a time, everything went by post and a fast efficient service depended on mail trains criss-crossing the country during the night. Dedicated post office carriages allowed letters and parcels to be sorted en route and delivered to their destination ready for the local delivery bag.

■ Postal workers sorting mail on a London Midland & Scottish Railway travelling post office, 1929.

■ The Travelling Post Office and the romance of the Night Mail have always struck a chord with the public. Here mail is loaded in readiness for its overnight journey. Photographed in 1960, the train is headed by ex-LMS Stanier 'Black Five' No.44877.

THE RAILWAYMEN– OFF THE TRAINS

Their work was gruelling and sometimes dangerous, but they had the satisfaction of knowing that they kept the railways running in tip-top condition.

Building the Engines

At the heart of the old steam railway were the great locomotive works where engines were built, but once they were in service it was a continual and highly skilled job involving thousands of men up and down the country to keep those engines in the best possible condition.

Engineer Richard Hardy recalled how his interest in engines began and how it led to a fascinating apprenticeship in the locomotive works during the war:

My first trip on the footplate was as a boy and the engine was a Sterling F1 built for the South Eastern Railway in about 1892, so in a sense I go back a very long way indeed! But that first trip gave me a love of engines that lasted through my working life and propelled me into railway work when I left school.

I went straight into a job as an engineering apprentice at Doncaster, I can remember the exact date – it was January 17, 1941. I started making motion pins and bolts for locomotives on a lathe – it was a wonderful training because everyone in the works from the highest to the lowest did their best and the parts they made were fitted together to make the engines that we took such pride in. The locomotive works were very strictly run in those early days too. You were expected to do as you were told and long hours and strict conditions were the norm. You were only paid when you came to work – I was not salaried in those days – and being late on duty was a serious matter. During my apprenticeship I was late once. I was going to work on my bike at 3am one moonlit Sunday morning when a policeman stopped me for not having a light – I was ten minutes late for work, lost half an hour's pay and was fined ten shillings.

■ PREVIOUS PAGE: GOING HOME; ENGINEMEN LEAVING THE DEPOT AT THE END OF THEIR SHIFT IN THE MID 1960S.

■ UNREBUILT 'WEST COUNTRY' CLASS 4-6-2 'LAPFORD' AND BR STANDARD CLASS '4MT' 2-6-0 76008 UNDERGO AN OVERHAUL AT EASTLEIGH WORKS ON 24 MAY 1966.

'... everyone in the works from the highest to the lowest did their best'

I believe I was the last premium apprentice on the LNER until after the war and those that followed me had the same training but without the premium. I always believed that an engineering apprenticeship is an education in engineering and in human relationships. It was all very autocratic in those days, but as I moved through the various engineering departments I discovered that the men I worked with never asked me to work harder than they were prepared and able to work themselves.

After the locomotive works I was sent to the running shed to learn how engines were maintained. It's important to remember the difference between the plant works, which was a factory, and the running shed. In the plant works, the discipline was rigid and production and output were the targets.

The running shed, with its endless movement of engines in steam, its drivers and firemen and its artisans, was less consistently busy, but then the scene would change and skilled men, fitters and boilermakers, could rise to amazing heights of endeavour to keep the traffic moving.

Working conditions in the plant and the running shed were very rough – no heating, for example, and no way to wash up except in a bucket of paraffin!

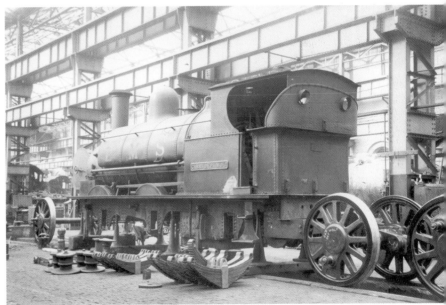

■ AN EX-SR 'SCHOOLS' CLASS 4-4-0 (TOP) RECEIVES ATTENTION AT EASTLEIGH WORKS IN AUGUST 1966.

■ A RAMSBOTTOM SPECIAL TANK, INTRODUCED IN 1870, UNDERGOING OVERHAUL AT ITS SPIRITUAL HOME IN CREWE IN LONDON MIDLAND & SCOTTISH DAYS. THESE ONCE WIDESPREAD LONDON & NORTH WESTERN RAILWAY SHUNTING ENGINES ENDED THEIR DAYS WITH FOUR OF THEIR NUMBER ALLOCATED TO WOLVERTON CARRIAGE WORKS.

Engineer Bill Sidwell started as an apprentice engineer at the Derby locomotive works. Day one saw him in the machine shop, in grease corner as it was known:

I was set to work putting threads on nuts – that's what everyone started on in those days. Everything seemed to be done in vast quantities of oil – at the end of the first week I was absolutely covered in the stuff! I moved around through the various departments and workshops – machine shop, boiler shop, erecting shop, foundry. This was where the practical work was done that kept the railway functioning. You wouldn't believe how tough that environment was – you needed to be physically strong because everywhere you looked massive pieces of machinery were being moved overhead and on the ground, or they were being machined and assembled, cleaned, polished or adjusted. It was all very dirty and very noisy, but at the end of the day you always felt you'd done something worthwhile, despite the fact that you were exhausted.

■ INCHICORE WORKS IN DUBLIN IN THE 1950S.

Nat Budgen was apprenticed as an engineer in Swindon and spent his working life there in some of the greatest railway workshops in the world:

Swindon was without doubt the greatest railway town in the country. I don't care what people say, we were the best – engines were built in those workshops from scratch and the men knew every nut and bolt, every rivet. These days people move jobs all the time and think there's something great about it – they think it's a good idea to move when you've found out what your job entails. That's the stupidest thing I've ever heard – when you've learned the ins and outs of the job, that's when you can start contributing, not before. Engineers at Swindon – and elsewhere I should imagine – only started to do the real work after years of learning on the job. And it really did take years, because they weren't going to let you mess around with the complicated stuff – metal that had to be lathed to very fine tolerances – until you could turn out easier jobs with your eyes closed.

Machine and parts making, fitting, assembly and repair were all a question of hard manual work and high technical skill – that's what people forget when they buy a diesel or electric engine today from a specialist manufacturer some place overseas. That lightweight electric engine has a finite life; it's made by robots and made to wear out. The engines we made and repaired were made to last forever. With maintenance they'd all be running today. Victorian engines were still running in the 1920s and in some cases I believe into the 1930s. We were making Rolls Royces, not the tinny little engines that drive the railways today. And no one I knew who had worked his way up at Swindon would have dreamed of leaving at any time – you were so pleased to get in as a lad that you knew you'd stay for life. There was nothing else in Swindon anyway, but Swindon was a railway town – it was built on the railways – and going into the workshops was a matter of pride. Local lads who didn't get in would try again and again because nothing else in Swindon packed the same punch. I'm proud I spent my working life there. I'm only sad that I've become a dinosaur. Most of my mates are dead now and when we've all gone it will be just like we were people who lived a thousand years ago, because the work we did is ancient history.

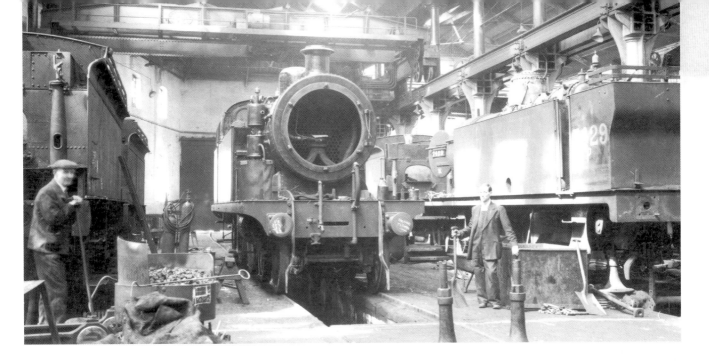

Until well into the British Rail era carriages were made using coachwork skills that would have been familiar to those who built the early stage coaches. Upholstery work was of the highest order and the timber parts of each carriage were made by craftsmen, as Arthur Archer recalled:

The GWR where I worked was amazing because it was self-contained – we made everything we needed, including our own tools for use in the workshops. I started work as a French polisher; all the woodwork in the carriages was cut and fitted and polished using the sort of skills you'd only really expect to see in a furniture workshop – and a hand-made one at that, because the woodwork in GWR carriages was superb. It was expected to be perfect because the GWR took pride in what it produced, down to the last pin and peg. The most impressive men in the carriageworks were the men who made the seats – the upholsterers. The cloth for carriage seats was of the highest quality – it had to be, to stand the wear and tear. And seats were stuffed so that despite years of sitting and rough use they didn't lose their shape. Those skills are gone now and seats are just replaced quickly when they wear out – even railway upholstery has become part of the throwaway world! And of course all the fine timberwork is gone – except perhaps on the dashboard of a Rolls Royce!

■ A RARE SCENE FROM BOW WORKS ON THE NORTH LONDON RAILWAY (TOP) WITH A LONDON TILBURY & SOUTHEND RAILWAY 4-4-2T AND AN LMS JINTY 0-6-0T RECEIVING OVERHAULS.

■ A BRITISH RAILWAYS WORKER CHECKS A SET OF LARGE DRIVING WHEELS (ABOVE) BEFORE THEY ARE FITTED TO A STEAM LOCOMOTIVE AT THE FORMER GWR WORKS AT SWINDON IN 1952.

■ WORKERS PAINTING THE EXTERIOR OF A NEW CARRIAGE (LEFT), POSSIBLY AT CREWE WORKS, IN 1945. AT THIS TIME AROUND 43,000 PEOPLE WERE EMPLOYED AT RAILWAY WORKS THROUGHOUT BRITAIN. HOW THINGS HAVE CHANGED!

J.W. Robertson Scott recalled an even more distant time in carriage building: *In my youth First Class carriages were made to represent three coach bodies joined together – I mean stage-coach bodies, and they were largely timber. At the end, outside, was a seat for the guard. Every railway had Second Class compartments. The earliest Second Class carriage, like the Third Class carriages, had no sides, the roof being supported by iron pillars. The passengers therefore suffered from wind and rain.*

The difference between freight wagons – loose coupled and without independent brakes – and passenger carriages, each with its own brakes, had to be taken into account by driver, fireman and guard.

From his time as a guard at King's Cross, Tom Jales remembered the dangers associated with freight wagons, which were crudely made and immensely strong:
I was working at Hornsey in north London at the time and the inspector told me to leave four coaches and release the engine. The carriages each had what was called a buck-eye coupling, which weighed about one hundredweight.

'The earliest Second Class carriage, like the Third Class carriages, had no sides, the roof being supported by iron pillars'

■ THE WHEEL SHOP AT THE MIDLAND RAILWAY'S DERBY WORKS.

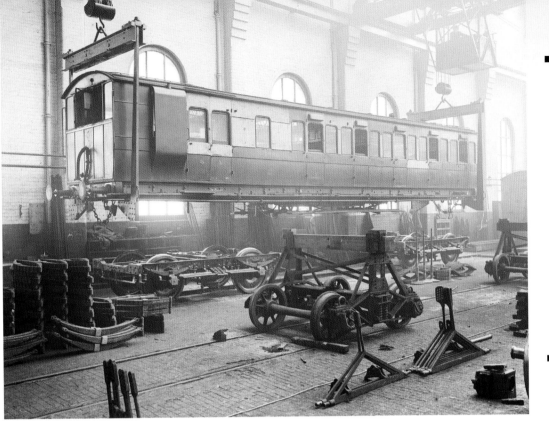

■ Carriage
manufacture at
the former London
& North Western
Railway's works
at Newton Heath
in Manchester in
1927. The works
closed in 1932.

■ Wooden carriage
construction at the
Midland Railway's
Derby Works in
1921.

You'd pull a chain and that would make the knuckle open; the two carriages would then move together and lock. That was the procedure. Anyway I was under this train setting the buck eye when the driver was told by the inspector that it was OK to reverse the train. I only just got out in time. It would have crushed my head like an eggshell!

But there was sadness too, as Arthur Archer recalled:

Too many people remember all the hard work in the foundry and machine shop, but I remember the sense that you were always among friends – you had your routine and were always greeted with warm smiles and a few cheeky jokes. It was like being in a big family and many men died soon after retiring, because without that family they felt lost.

REFUELLING

Delivering the essential ingredients for the production of steam – coal and water – huge mechanical coaling plants and curiously shaped water hoses were once as common a sight on the railway network as footbridges and signal boxes.

- STANIER 'BLACK FIVE' (RIGHT) 4-6-0 NO.44962 BEING COALED AT SPRINGS BRANCH (WIGAN) SHED ON 29 JUNE 1966.

- SCENE AT RAMSGATE SHED (BELOW) WITH A MAUNSELL 'SCHOOLS' CLASS 4-4-0 TAKING COAL. ON THE RIGHT A CLASS 'H' 0-4-4T AND A CLASS 'T9' 4-4-0 COMPLETE THIS PRE-WAR VIEW.

- EX-GWR '14XX' CLASS 0-4-2T NO.1420 (BOTTOM) MARSHALS A TINY FREIGHT TRAIN AT REMOTE PRESTEIGNE, WALES, IN SEPTEMBER 1964 WHILE THE LOCAL COAL MERCHANT'S LORRY STANDS IN FRONT OF THE STATION.

- A TRIPLE EX-GWR LINEUP (ABOVE) AT GLOUCESTER HORTON ROAD ENGINE SHED ON 2 MAY 1964 – FROM LEFT TO RIGHT 2-6-2T NO.4564, 2-6-0 NO.6349 AND 0-4-2T NO.1474.

- EX-WAR DEPARTMENT RIDDLES 'AUSTERITY' CLASS 2-8-0 NO.90495 (FAR LEFT) TAKES WATER AT WEST HARTLEPOOL SHED DURING THE EARLY 1960S.

- THE BITTER WINTER COLDNESS IS ELOQUENTLY PORTRAYED (LEFT), AS ARE THE RIGOURS OF STEAM LOCOMOTIVE OPERATIONS, IN THIS PHOTOGRAPH OF A STANIER 'BLACK FIVE' 4-6-0 TAKING ON WATER AT SKIPTON, NORTH YORKSHIRE, IN THE 1960S.

*'... the
trickiest
bit of the
permanent
way was
designing
the curves
on the rails'*

■ REMOVING SIGNAL
GANTRIES AT
CHURCHDOWN ON
THE GLOUCESTER TO
CHELTENHAM MAIN
LINE, 26 FEBRUARY
1967.

The Track Works

**Keeping the track in good order has always been vital – we've seen the
results of neglecting the permanent way in recent dreadful accidents – but
the old steam railway had the manpower to ensure remarkably high levels
of maintenance.**

Stationmaster Cliff Carr recalled the difficult conditions in which the
permanent way staff sometimes had to work:
*Nantybwch in our remote part of Wales was famous for its dreadful winter
weather – so much so that the permanent way staff were sometimes on snow
and frost duty for weeks on end, and on one never-to-be-forgotten day a pile
of huge stones fell from a bridge a few miles from the station and almost
derailed a train. For six weeks after that buses were used while the bridge was
demolished and rebuilt.*

LNER driver Allan Richardson remembered the rules and regulations:
*You received a book each week with the temporary speed restrictions on
various roads. This – the Permanent Way Notice – was known among the men
by its nickname – the Navvy. That name probably hadn't changed in more
than a century and it referred to the fact that it was the navvies who built the
permanent way – the track, embankments and bridges.*

■ A Signal & Telegraph open-air smithy (right) at Whitland Station in Cardigan, 24 August 1972.

Engineer Ken Williams remembered the complexity of working on the permanent way:

The assistant district engineer told me I was to be in charge of permanent way and the trickiest bit of the permanent way was designing the curves on the rails. Whatever you might think, curves are not as simple as they look and they go very easily out of alignment. It isn't like a model railway where you have a straight bit of track and you simply add a curve to it. In the real world the straight bit has gradually to curve into the curved bit, if you see what I mean. It's actually very complex. Basically how we used to do it was to mark the curve into 66-foot sections (66 feet was what we called a chain, by the way), then we'd get a string and let it span between the 66-foot interval points. You'd then measure the distance from string to rail and plot the shape of the curve.

When you'd mapped the thing out, the platelayers would quite literally push the track until it was exactly where you wanted it. Some curves had to be looked at every month, particularly if it was a curve over which the trains were going fast. Each district had a certain amount of track that had to be renewed each year so someone had to organize things so the gangs and equipment were ready and in the right place at the right time.

■ In stark contrast to today's stringent rules and regulations regarding high visibility vests, hard hats, safety footware and lookouts, these workers show a more relaxed and unregulated attitude to their work as they build a new platform at a station in South East London in the 1950s.

Signalmen

Today trains are monitored and controlled from sophisticated electronic central control rooms. In the steam era it was very different and much of the responsibility for safety rested on the shoulders of the signalmen – highly trained individuals often working alone and in remote locations up and down the country.

George Case, who started as a telegraph lad just after the war began, recalled:

It was accepted practice that the telegraph lad would operate the levers while the signalman had his breakfast. This was all a bit unofficial, but it wasn't difficult, because the signalman was always on hand if you got stuck and it didn't take long anyway to become familiar with the way the system worked.

Mind you, there was a knack to pulling those levers – they weren't power-assisted or anything so you had to put your weight behind them. Distant signals were more difficult because they were farther off, obviously, and down below the cabin were the rods and linkages that led off up or down the track, so if you were moving a signal a good distance away you were moving a lot of metal, although counterbalancing weights were fitted to make things a little easier. Some points were particularly difficult – first you had to unlock them, then get clearance (i.e. prove that nothing was on that bit of track), then you had to open the bar point lock; this was a lock lever that kept the points where you wanted them. Only then could you go ahead.

■ A VIEW OF THE INTERIOR OF CHURCHDOWN SIGNAL BOX ON THE GLOUCESTER TO CHELTENHAM LINE IN NOVEMBER 1966. THE SIGNALMAN SEEN HERE, PERCY WILLIAMS, RETIRED WHEN THE BOX WAS CLOSED IN FEBRUARY 1967.

Signalboxes were almost like closed worlds, with rules of their own, and the signalman and his telegraph lad, if he had one, had to be self-sufficient. There was a stove for heating up tea and even meals and there were chemical loos.

David Evans had similar memories but also recalled the huge responsibilities of even the youngest recruit:

As a young recruit you went straight into a signals cabin where you first learned to fill in the train registration book. In a busy box you'd have four pages of booking per shift. Each line of entry in the book had ten items that had to be filled in – the time the train was offered, the time it was accepted, time passed on, time passing in the rear and so on. It worked out at ten items per line, 40 lines per page – a total of 400 items per page, and there were four pages per shift.

That was a hell of a lot of entries for a young lad. For the early shift I had to be there at 6am and if you were the least bit late the boss knew straight away because the bookings would not be there and, of course, you couldn't add them after the event.

Harry Horn down in Somerset recalled the hardships of the signalman's life in bad weather in the 1930s:

Each signalman had a sign a specified number of yards distant from his box and if he could no longer see it because of fog he telephoned for the fog signalman. All engineers might be mobilized for this work – they all had their allocated places for when the need arose. It was the same with snow duty; every man had his allotted place in an emergency to clear the points, which got horribly jammed by snow. In really bad weather you might have to stand all day by a set of points.

■ AN EARLY VIEW OF WILLESDEN No.9 SIGNALBOX (ABOVE LEFT) ON THE L&NWR MAIN LINE OUT OF EUSTON.

■ THE DRIVER OF A HEREFORD TO GLOUCESTER TRAIN (ABOVE RIGHT) EXCHANGES HIS SINGLE LINE TOKEN AT GRANGE COURT JUNCTION, 25 APRIL 1964.

'It was accepted practice that the telegraph lad would operate the levers while the signalman had his breakfast'

Harry also recalled the atmosphere and occasional terrors of signal work:

My instructor was a marvellous chap and we got on very well. I was trained for six weeks on Saturdays only. Then I was sent to a signalbox at Charwelton in Oxfordshire to watch a signalman at work and learn the bell codes. We had an up and a down line, a refuse siding, goods yard and a little branch line to an iron-ore mine.

Charwelton was the signalbox near the Catesby Tunnel, which runs for 3,000 yards. The regulations here were stricter than they would normally have been, because of the tunnel, and one hour into my first day in the box there was an emergency. The emergency bell went and we discovered that the down freight had dropped a door. It gave me a fright, but I had the experienced signalman with me so I learned a lot by seeing how to deal with a crisis so early in my time.

Working in the signalbox was a lonely life in some ways but we had old omnibus phones and we used to talk to each other – the signalmen I mean. On the Rugby to Woodford line there were seven boxes and it was a very busy line for freight. There was seldom what we called a clear block – that is, a time when no trains were moving.

I worked all the boxes from Charwelton (a class 4 box) to Woodford 1, then to Woodford 3 (a class 2 box). Class 1 was the busiest, class 5 the least busy.

For many men whose hearts had been set on driving, the move to the signalbox could have been a blow from which it would have been difficult to recover, but for Harry it had its compensations. It was a place of quiet routine but that routine was occasionally interrupted by moments of drama and even danger:

Yes, there were occasional dramas – apart from the odd horse getting loose once in a while and stopping all the trains, I can remember one night

■ THE ELEGANT NORTH EASTERN RAILWAY SIGNAL BOX AND FOOTBRIDGE AT HALTWHISTLE STATION ON THE NEWCASTLE TO CARLISLE LINE IN 1967.

■ A SINGLE-LINE TOKEN EXCHANGE AT HAVENSTREET STATION ON THE ISLE OF WIGHT LINE FROM RYDE TO COWES IN AUGUST 1965.

DICKENS AND STEAM

Steam engines appear frequently in Dickens's fiction, often at moments of high drama or tragedy: in the short story 'The Signalman', a signalman is killed by a train, following a series of supernatural warnings. Dickens himself experienced the Staplehurst rail crash of 9 June, 1865. While passing over a viaduct in Kent, the train jumped a gap in the line and several carriages fell on to the riverbed below. Dickens was in the only First Class carriage to survive.

at 2am when, as you can imagine, it was normally as quiet as the grave, I heard footsteps on the steps outside the box. It gave me a fright but it was only a soldier looking for a ride. I told him to go to Woodford and catch the night mail.

Reg Holmes, working in a remote signal box in rural Cheshire, recalled the arduousness of the work:

Well I think people would be surprised, for example, at just how much effort it took to pull on the levers that operated the distant signals. Just the weight of the wire on a signal half a mile away took some shifting. I think the best way to pull involved getting your weight behind the lever rather than using brute force, but it was definitely an art that took some time to acquire. I remember when the late Poet Laureate John Betjeman visited my box – he was very keen on the old railways – he tried to pull one of the distant levers and couldn't do it at all!

■ SEMAPHORES GALORE - THE GROUND FLOOR OF READING SIGNAL YARD STORES PHOTOGRAPHED ON 22 MAY 1950.

'John Betjeman visited my box – he was very keen on the old railways'

MAINTENANCE

Engines working constantly at high pressures and temperatures hauling heavy loads in all conditions meant that constant maintenance was required. It was heavy work that required strength and stamina as well as skill and experience.

■ STANIER 'BLACK FIVE' 4-6-0 NO.45350 BEING TURNED AT NEWTON HEATH SHED ON 8 JUNE 1968.

■ THE PERIODIC WASHING OUT OF STEAM LOCOMOTIVE BOILERS IN ORDER TO REMOVE HARMFUL SLUDGE AND DEPOSITS WAS NECESSARY TO MAINTAIN PEAK PERFORMANCE.

■ PRESERVED EX-LNER 'A3' 4-6-2 NO.4472 (ABOVE LEFT) 'FLYING SCOTSMAN' BEING PREPARED AT SOUTHALL SHED ON 7 OCTOBER 1965 FOR A SPECIAL TRAIN THE NEXT DAY.

■ GRESLEY'S V2 CLASS 2-6-2 NO.60845 (FAR LEFT) SPENT A CONSIDERABLE AMOUNT OF TIME ON EXTENSIVE TESTING AT SWINDON WORKS DURING THE 1950S. HERE, THE LOCOMOTIVE IS PUT THROUGH ITS PACES ON THE ROLLING ROAD.

■ A FITTER AT ROSE GROVE SHED IN BURNLEY (LEFT) GIVES LAST MINUTE ATTENTION TO AN EX-LMS STANIER CLASS '8F' 2-8-0 DURING THE LAST FEW MONTHS OF STEAM ON BRITISH RAILWAYS.

RAILWAY DISASTERS

The 19th century welcomed the railway as a symbol of technological advance. But the enormous scale of destruction involved in the admittedly rare rail accidents has remained a source of great concern into our own times.

■ THIS DERAILMENT ON THE MIDLAND RAILWAY OUTSIDE WELLINGBOROUGH STATION ON 2 SEPTEMBER 1898 LED TO SEVEN FATALITIES.

■ ONE OF THE WORST HEAD-ON COLLISIONS IN BRITISH RAILWAY HISTORY OCCURRED ON 10 SEPTEMBER 1874 WHEN TWO GREAT EASTERN RAILWAY TRAINS COLLIDED BETWEEN NORWICH THORPE AND BRUNDALL STATIONS.

■ ON 15 OCTOBER 1907 A LONDON & NORTH WESTERN RAILWAY MAIL TRAIN DERAILED AT HIGH SPEED (ABOVE AND NEAR LEFT) AT SHREWSBURY STATION. IN THE RESULTANT ACCIDENT 18 PEOPLE WERE KILLED. THE LOCOMOTIVE INVOLVED WAS 'EXPERIMENT' CLASS 4-6-0 'STEPHENSON'.

■ IN COUNTY DURHAM, ON 24 OCTOBER 1905 (FAR LEFT), TWO NORTH EASTERN RAILWAY 0-6-0 LOCOMOTIVES WERE DERAILED BY A MISSING LENGTH OF RAIL BETWEEN WINSTON AND GAINFORTH.

■ THE WORST PEACETIME RAIL CRASH OCCURRED AT HARROW & WEALDSTONE STATION ON 8 OCTOBER 1952 WHEN 112 PEOPLE WERE KILLED AND 340 INJURED. THE CRASH INVOLVED THREE TRAINS.

All Aboard! – Staffing the Station

Most travellers' memories of the steam era agree that stations were wonderfully well staffed compared to more recent times. The big city stations were crowded with porters and telegram boys, ticket collectors, guards and other staff.

Smaller stations were carefully manned too but there were differences: staff often had to double up on their duties, for example, as signalman George Case remembered:

At Crews Hill I had what was called a porter signalman's job - in other words it was a tiny station where you virtually did a bit of everything: signals, booking clerk, stationmaster, porter. And the stationmaster looked after two other stations! In fact there wasn't much signal work to be done – you only really opened up the cabin to shorten the block or to perform shunting duties.

But at many stations staff camaraderie was strong and lifelong friendships were made, as South Wales stationmaster Cliff Carr recalled:

Eardisley was a small country station and I arrived knowing no one in the area, in November 1947. It was freezing and I had a long walk into the village, for the station was well outside Eardisley itself. But you would have to go a long way to meet a man as nice as dear Ernie Brooks who was to be my stationmaster. He was about 60 when I first met him at Eardisley. He was a real old-style railwayman, friendly and helpful and really one of the nicest chaps I've ever worked with.

■ TWO VERY CHEERFUL AND SMARTLY DRESSED STAFF AT ALTON IN HAMPSHIRE IN THE EARLY DAYS OF BRITISH RAILWAYS.

Ernie and I were the only clerical staff at Eardisley, although there were also signalmen and porters and goods staff; but we were also responsible for keeping an eye on Kinnersley Station and Whitney-on-Wye, both local stations. I can recall rushing between the three stations pretty regularly! I had to deal with passenger, goods and parcel traffic, and I remember thinking at the time that clerical work at small country stations gave you an insight into how railways really worked – it was as if you could see the structure on which everything else was based. We used to book tickets for passengers and organize the

6757 A

"THE LOST TICKET."

ROTARY PHOTO, E.C.

GENERAL
WAITING ROOM

work in the goods office, dealing mostly with farm
produce – grain, hay, sugar beet and so on.

Together with his stationmaster, Cliff was
responsible for paying 20 men in the area – these
included platelayers, maintenance men, station
repairers, signalmen and shunters. They also paid
themselves:
*We certainly did, but like everything else it was all
checked by the district office – everything in those
days was recorded, checked and double-checked.*

J.W. Robertson Scott remembered the small
country stations of his youth:
*A country station was like a small village. It
might have half a dozen staff, each at a different
grade and each allotted certain specific tasks. As
promotion was largely based on seniority there
was no bad feeling or sense that some clever dick
might come in above another member of staff who
had worked for years learning the job. Experience
was everything on the old railway – part of
the mess the modern railway got itself into was
caused by abandoning this old system and opting
for management consultants and others with no
knowledge of how railways work.*

■ A LONDON MIDLAND & SCOTTISH RAILWAY
PORTER PREPARING TO CLEAN THE GENERAL
WAITING ROOM AT HATCH END STATION IN
1937.

The Railwaymen – off the Trains **217**

Health, Wealth and Welfare –
Railwaymen's Clubs and Recreation

**In the days of the big four railway companies and on into the British Rail
era the social life of the railwaymen – and women – was closely allied to
their working life.**

THE RAILWAY MISSION

The Railway Mission was formed
in 1881 to communicate the gospel
to those working on and around
the railways. It built several chapels
across the country, but few now
survive; the Prince of Wales Road
Evangelical Church in Norwich, built
in the 1890s, is one of a few still in
use. The Mission's work continues
today, serving the rail network and
the British Transport Police.

Social clubs were common as well as savings clubs, whether for holidays,
retirement or funerals. Much of this side of life was organized and run by the
railway unions, as driver Reg Coote recalled:

*I was always keen on the union and was for many years assistant branch
secretary for Battersea. We used to organize dinner dances and a big kids'
party every Christmas. The children's party was held in a big listed building in
Vauxhall in central London – the Brunswick Building, which is still there. I
can remember carting hundreds of party hats and jellies around the streets of
south London in a mate's old car and being terrified we might squash the hats
and the cakes! But the kids loved it – and remember, railwaymen, like most
working men, weren't paid a lot. We had to club together to help each other
and to give our children a bit of fun – no foreign holidays in those days and
precious little help from the companies we worked for.*

One of Reg's most poignant memories is of the solidarity of railwaymen at difficult times:

We stood up for each other when things were hard and helped the widows and orphans of dead colleagues. Funerals of colleagues were treated with great respect and woe betide a man who failed to do his bit.

When a driver died in the steam days his mates always formed the pallbearers. They carried the coffin out of his house to the horse-drawn hearse – everyone insisted on horses in those days – and the whole street came out to see the coffin away. The chapel would be packed out with his mates too. I remember old Bill Cook died at Stewarts Lane and you couldn't move in the church. That sort of thing faded with the coming of the electric and then diesel.

The best way to illustrate the change is probably to compare the way we made collections for the dead man's widow at the start of my career and the way we had to do it towards the end of my time. In the old days when a man died we'd leave a tin out in the lobby to collect money for the relatives. No one would have dreamt of doing anything other than adding to the amount already in the tin, but towards the end we had to stop doing it because all the money got stolen.

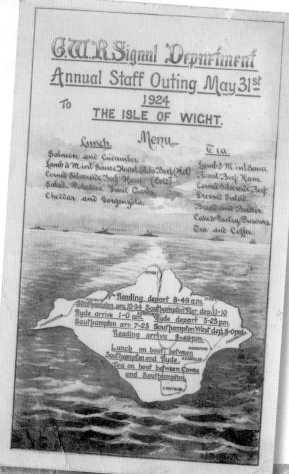

■ THE GWR LOOKED AFTER ITS STAFF! HERE, THE SIGNAL DEPARTMENT ARE INVITED ON THEIR ANNUAL STAFF OUTING TO THE ISLE OF WIGHT IN 1924.

■ MEN, YOUNG AND OLD, POSE FOR THE CAMERA AS THEY LEAVE SWINDON WORKS AT THE END OF THEIR SHIFT.

■ TWO STANIER 'BLACK FIVES' AND AN '8F' LURK IN PATRICROFT ENGINE SHED ON 15 JUNE 1968, ONLY ABOUT SIX WEEKS BEFORE THE END OF STEAM ON BRITISH RAILWAYS.

■ UN-REBUILT BULLEID PACIFIC NO.34102, 'LAPFORD', A REGULAR PERFORMER BETWEEN WEYMOUTH AND WATERLOO IN THE FINAL YEARS OF SOUTHERN MAIN LINE STEAM, IS SEEN HERE UNDER REPAIR AT BOURNEMOUTH MPD.

ENGINE SHEDS

For any trainspotter, the engine shed was an Aladdin's cave offering the chance to see any number of cherished locomotives at close quarters. Gaining access, however, was not always easy.

■ THE HANDSOME CONTOURS OF THE BR STANDARD CLASS 5MT 4-6-0 ARE REVEALED IN THIS SHED SCENE. NOTICE THE ENGINE ARRANGEMENT BOARD IN THE BACKGROUND. THESE BOARDS CARRIED UP TO THE MINUTE INFORMATION ON LOCOMOTIVE WORKING DIAGRAMS.

■ WEYMOUTH ENGINE SHED ON 21 AUGUST 1966.

■ ALL HANDS TO THE MILL AS A STANIER BR STANDARD CLASS 4-6-0 IS TURNED ON THE TURNTABLE READY FOR ITS NEXT TURN OF DUTY.

HOLIDAYS BY RAIL

The railways caused profound and lasting changes to British society, as they brought travel for enjoyment into the reach of ordinary people for the first time.

Made by Rail – Resorts and Destinations

The idea of going to the seaside for a holiday developed almost entirely as a result of the ever-expanding railway. Indeed many seaside towns owe their growth and prosperity – in some cases their very existence – to railway travel.

Tom Shackle remembered the pre-eminent holiday railway – the Great Western:

The GWR was always seen as the holiday railway because it served the West Country – land of wide beaches and glorious weather. Towns like Sidmouth, Swanage and Weymouth grew rapidly after the arrival of the railway – they became rich in fact – and when I was a boy we still went every year, as people had done in the late 19th century when the hotels and seafront houses were built to accommodate the summer arrivals.

We always went to Weymouth, which you can see from its lovely seafront houses grew up in the 19th century to cater for all the holidaymakers – people like my family who stayed in the same boarding-house overlooking the sea year after year. I remember breakfast, which we all had in the dining room, and the long days in the sun on the beach. All of it was exciting – from the journey down by train from London to the walks along the coast. The Great Western Railway even published books on the holiday towns they could take you to, and they were best sellers; one was called Holiday Heaven. *And it was the same in the southern region – in the 1830s only a few thousand people a year went to Brighton, but by the 1840s more than 300,000 went in the summer months alone!*

■ THE LISKEARD TO LOOE TRAIN CROSSES WITH THE EX-GWR 2-6-2T IN AUGUST 1959.

■ THE NEWLY POPULAR SEASIDE RESORT OF BLACKPOOL WAS SERVED BY SPECIAL TRAINS PULLED BY ENGINES SUCH AS THE STANIER 'BLACK FIVE' 4-6-0 No.45076, SHOWN HERE.

■ A MIXED BAG OF GWR CARRIAGES HEADS ALONG THE SEAFRONT AT DAWLISH IN THE EARLY 20TH CENTURY.

In East Anglia the coast developed in a similar way, as stationmaster Rod Lock recalled:

At Swaffham in Norfolk before the war the trains were packed in summer with families going to the coastal resorts that had grown up to meet the demand – the railway staff used to get caught up in their excitement. This was in the days before foreign holidays left the same seaside resorts in serious decline. Cromer and places like it went from being tiny impoverished fishing villages to being bustling holiday resorts within a generation – and all thanks to the railway.

■ A PLETHORA OF BRITISH RAILWAYS HOLIDAY POSTERS, RANGING FROM THE ISLES OF SCILLY TO THE WEST HIGHLAND LINE, GREETED PASSENGERS AT BUILTH ROAD (LOW LEVEL) IN THE SUMMER OF 1962.

THE LURE OF SEA AIR

In 1871, Skegness, Lincolnshire, had a population of less than 500. In 1873 a railway line was opened and a large station built. The idea was to tempt holidaymakers to the town's sandy beaches – and it worked. Tourists came and the town's infrastructure quickly grew. By 1907 Skegness boasted 300,000 visitors a year, largely from the industrial towns of the East Midlands and Yorkshire.

Trains ran to resorts all along the west Norfolk coast at a time when private cars were still the preserve of the few. I think the sense of community died a bit when cars started to be used because people became more independent, and then foreign holidays killed the holiday coast trains completely, and that in turn meant the boarding-houses and hotels gradually became shabby and run down and awful, which they were in the 1970s. But I think there's been a revival of interest in English seaside holidays in more recent years, though it will never go back to what it was in the 1950s.

Harry Horn working in Somerset recalled:

Electricity and mains water finally came to Stogumber in the 1960s when the future of small rural railways was already under a cloud. But business was still pretty good and at Stogumber, as at many stations, we even had railway carriages in sidings that had been fitted out with beds and kitchens for rent to holidaymakers!

The Minehead-Taunton line survived the Beeching Cuts – it was the only branch line he left in the West Country – because it had been the making of Butlins holiday camp at Minehead, and the holiday camp continued to generate enough traffic to justify keeping the line open for passengers if not freight until 1971.

- EX-GWR 'HALL' CLASS 4-6-0 NO.4991 (RIGHT) 'COBHAM HALL' LEAVES DAWLISH WARREN WITH A LOCAL TRAIN FOR PAIGNTON ON 9 AUGUST 1956.

- A CAMBRIAN RAILWAYS POSTCARD OF 1906 USED TO REQUEST ACCOMMODATION AND TRAVEL INFORMATION BY POTENTIAL HOLIDAYMAKERS.

- A GREAT WESTERN RAILWAY RAILMOTOR DISCHARGES ITS PASSENGERS AT DAWLISH WARREN STATION, IN SOUTH DEVON.

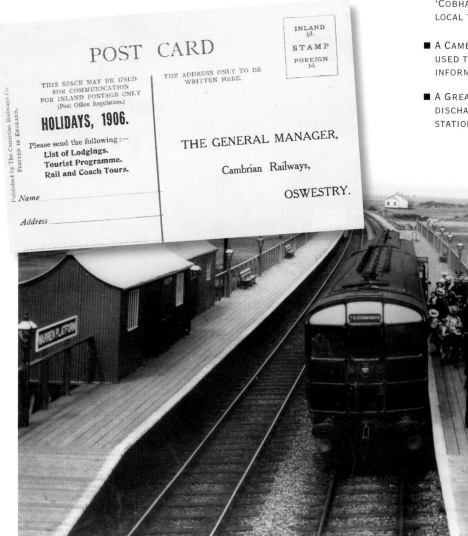

Harry Horn also recalled how much pleasure Minehead gave to the tens of thousands who flocked there over the years:

Minehead and the railway that served it were like two parts of the same holiday – the fact that trains could get a lot of people to what had been a remote place transformed it. I remember children and adults leaning out of the windows all excited that they were on holiday and they still leaned out as the trains moved slowly off – wouldn't be allowed now I know, but it's a picture that has stayed in my head. And of course as fast as the packed trains went to Minehead in one direction other trains were coming back and bringing holidaymakers home again in the other direction. The railway thrived on it, as did the town, but it could never ultimately compete with the lure of foreign holidays. That was and is the tragedy of the English seaside resort.

■ THROUGHOUT THE MIDDLE YEARS OF THE 20TH CENTURY BRITISH TOURISTS BOUND FOR BUTLIN'S HOLIDAY CAMPS POURED OFF TRAINS EVERY SUMMER. THE RAILWAYS, WHICH PROVIDED EASY ACCESS TO THE CAMPS, WERE AN IMPORTANT INGREDIENT IN THEIR SUCCESS.

Beside the Seaside – day-trippers

Holidays were almost unheard of before the arrival of the railway, for the simple reason that travel was too expensive and since hardly anyone went anywhere businesses, such as hotels and guest-houses, didn't exist to cater for them. But with the arrival of the train even the poorest could occasionally afford a day out, and in a small country like Britain the favourite destination was the seaside. Indeed the seaside special became something of an institution and finally disappeared only with the advent of cheaper foreign travel in the 1960s.

Rose Plummer remembers seaside trips that were the highlight of her youth:
We didn't have any of the expensive sophisticated holidays people have today so when we decided on a seaside day it was something to look forward to – children would be mad with excitement for weeks before and their mums would make loads of food to eat on the train and on the beach or pier. They took their food with them because even a day trip by train was likely to cost a poor East End family more than they could really afford, so they had no extra money for cafés and shops.

'... places like it went from being tiny impoverished fishing villages to being bustling holiday resorts'

■ EXCURSION ADVERTISEMENTS AT NORTHAMPTON FOR THE TOWN'S ANNUAL HOLIDAY PERIOD 1957.

■ A THRONG OF DAY-TRIPPERS ARRIVE AT BLACKPOOL CENTRAL STATION IN THE EARLY 20TH CENTURY.

BRITISH RAILWAYS

NORTHAMPTON TOWN HOLIDAYS 1957
ADDITIONAL THROUGH TRAINS — *From:* NORTHAMPTON CASTLE SATURDAY 27 JULY

12·45 A.M. PORTSMOUTH	6·15 A.M. BLACKPOOL	6·50 A.M. LLANDUDNO
5·30 A.M. } LONDON EUSTON	6·30 A.M. SCARBOROUGH	7·5 A.M. BRIGHTON
5·30 A.M. MARGATE	6·47 A.M. } YARMOUTH	8·30 A.M. HASTINGS

■ THE OVERHEAD
ELECTRIFICATION ON
THIS PICTURE DEFINES
THE LOCATION AS
SHEFFIELD, FROM
WHICH A CITY OF
LEICESTER HOLIDAY
SPECIAL DEPARTS
— IN ALL PROBABILITY
FOR BLACKPOOL. IT
IS HAULED BY A 'B17
SANDRINGHAM CLASS'
4-6-0.

■ THIS GREAT
NORTHERN RAILWAY
POSTER ADVERTISING
THE BRACING SEA AIR
OF SKEGNESS HAS
BECOME AN ICON OF
THE LAST CENTURY.

I remember going from Liverpool Street to Southend and waving from the
window to people I didn't even know as we left – I just wanted to wave
to anyone really, I was so excited. You can't lean out the window and wave
today – the windows don't open any more and it wouldn't be allowed by
Health and Safety!

When I was young us kids would be in the compartments jumping up
and down and some families would have started on their food as they left
the station – the noise and chatter was deafening, like the noise on the old
hop specials that took the families down to Kent for six weeks picking in the
summer. Like the seaside specials those hop trains were still going in the early
1960s – hard to believe it but it's true!

When we got to Southend we'd all pour out of the station and down to
the pier where we got another little train out a mile to the end of the pier.
Then it was ice creams and 'What the Butler Saw' machines all day. We
didn't really mind if it rained, it was all so different from all our other days.
I think Butlins really killed the day-trippers' seaside special. But things
change, don't they? You just have to accept it, and though the seaside specials
were fun it was just one day, and when we could have a cheap one-week
holiday instead we did.

Holidays by Rail 229

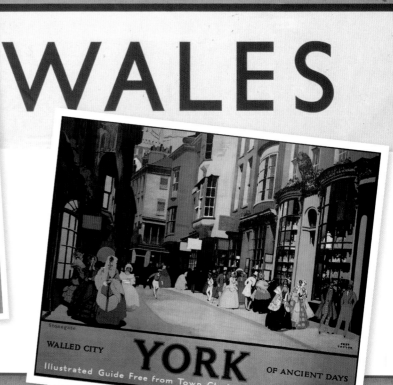

WALES

THE CALEDONIAN RAILWAY

THE "TRUE LINE" IS
THE SHORTEST SPACE BETWEEN
TWO POINTS AND WHETHER YOU
TRAVEL BY IT ON BUSINESS TO
TOWN OR CITY OR
TOUR FOR HEALTH OR PLEASURE
TO LOVELY LANDS OR
TO SILVERY SEA
THE TRAIN WILL
TAKE YOU FAR AND NEAR WITH
TRUE CONVENIENCE.
TRUE COMFORT. AND
TRUE DELIGHT
TO THE TUNE OF
TRUE ECONOMY AND
TO THE RHYTHM OF
TRUE TO TIME.
TRUE TO TIME.
TRUE TO TIME.

WALLED CITY YORK OF ANCIENT DAYS
Illustrated Guide Free from Town Clerk or any L·N·E·R Agency

HOLIDAY POSTERS

The railways opened up new possibilities for tourism all over the country and the railway companies were only too keen to encourage people to buy a ticket with glamorous and inviting depictions of their resorts and destinations

- TOM PURVIS'S NAÏVE AND COLOURFUL LNER POSTER FOR BRIDLINGTON WAS IMMEDIATELY ATTRACTIVE TO PARENTS OF YOUNG CHILDREN IN 1935.

- ALFRED LAMBART'S 1937 GWR POSTER FOR NEWQUAY (BELOW LEFT) APPEALS TO THE VIGOROUS HEDONISM OF A GENERATION THAT WAS TO BE DECIMATED BY THE COMING WAR.

- ALEC FRASER'S C1919 GWR POSTER FOR THE QUEEN'S HOTEL IN PENZANCE (BELOW RIGHT) IS DIRECTED AT A MORE STAID CLIENTELE.

- LEONARD RICHMOND'S 1930S JOINT GWR/LMS POSTER (ABOVE) CAPTURES THE IDYLLIC BEAUTY OF THE WELSH LANDSCAPE.

- A CALEDONIAN RAILWAY POSTER (FAR LEFT) EXTOLLING THE VIRTUES OF TRAVEL ON ITS TRAINS VERGES ON POETRY.

- A NOSTALGIC VIEW OF 19TH CENTURY YORK (LEFT) IN THIS LNER POSTER PAINTED BY FRED TAYLOR, 1930.

'... it seemed a marvel to me that the train pulled in and it was then just a short walk to the boat'

Taking the Boat Train

The old boat trains were loved by both drivers and passengers – the latter always excited since they were heading for exotic places, the former because they knew that they were working on some of the railway companies' most important routes.

Reg Coote fired on the Golden Arrow boat service for many years after the war ended:

I loved the Golden Arrow locos because they had some interesting peculiarities – in fact they were all individuals, but top quality and well serviced because they were carrying passengers to cross the Channel. But most of all I enjoyed driving the boat trains on the Ostend route – you just felt like the élite of the élite! By 1961 they'd electrified the Ostend boat train and the Golden Arrow had become an electric engine. At first the electric seemed great – so clean after steam and you got better shifts, but it changed the whole atmosphere of the thing.

■ PASSENGERS FOR TRANSATLANTIC LINERS WERE CONVEYED
FROM LONDON IN SPECIAL BOAT TRAINS RUN BY THE GREAT
WESTERN RAILWAY, LONDON & SOUTH WESTERN RAILWAY
AND THE LONDON & NORTH WESTERN RAILWAY.

■ THE GREAT WESTERN RAILWAY RAN FAST BOAT
TRAINS FROM PADDINGTON TO FISHGUARD TO
CONNECT WITH THEIR FERRY ROUTE TO ROSSLARE
IN IRELAND.

GREAT WESTERN RAILWAY.
The Direct Route to
IRELAND
via FISHGUARD

Magnificently appointed
TURBINE STEAMERS, 22½ Knots.
Sea Passage under 3 Hours.
PADDINGTON STATION, W.   JAMES C. INGLIS, GEN. MANAGER.
ANDREW REID & CO., LTD., GREY ST., NEWCASTLE.

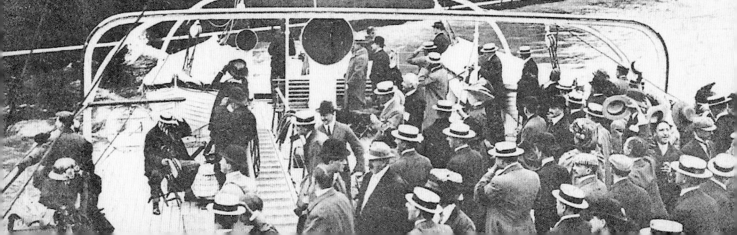

"PASSENGER TENDER
LEAVING R.M.S. "MAURETANIA."

Tom Shackle recalled his grandfather's comments about boat trains:

He used to tell me that in Kent they were the really lucrative lines because they carried travellers to the steam ships that were themselves owned by the railway company – and of course travellers from abroad had to get to London from the port at Dover, so it was always busy and they tended to use their best carriages and engines.

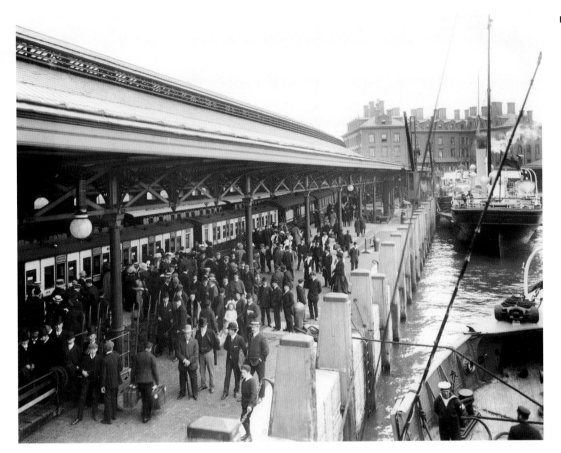

■ PASSENGERS FROM
IRELAND DISEMBARK
FROM 'SS CEDRIC' AT
HOLYHEAD TO JOIN A
WAITING BOAT TRAIN
FOR LONDON IN 1909.

■ A DINING CAR ON A
LONDON & NORTH
WESTERN RAILWAY
AMERICAN BOAT TRAIN
IN 1908.

Sheila Kehoe's family memories go back a long way – in fact to the period when boat trains ran to Southampton for the Atlantic crossing:

You were treated as very special – my father used to say that the GWR boat trains ran faster than any others and if a boat was expected an extra train or two might be put on to bring the passengers to London or to take them down to the coast from London.

But my strongest memories are of boat trains to Holyhead – it was the standard way to Ireland before cheap flights. The carriages and compartments were nothing special, but it seemed a marvel to me that the train pulled in and it was then just a short walk to the boat – with your bags carried by a helpful porter. I can remember, too, that as late as 1963 the train to Holyhead from London was still pulled by a steam engine.

The Channel Ports and Beyond

■ SEEN HERE HAULED BY A BR 'BRITANNIA' CLASS 4-6-2 IN 1957, THE 'GOLDEN ARROW' WAS A 1ST CLASS PULLMAN TRAIN THAT CONVEYED PASSENGERS FROM LONDON VICTORIA TO PARIS.

Before cheap air travel the only way to get to the Continent for most people was via the Channel ports, and as foreign travellers tended to be well off, the railway companies made special efforts on their behalf.

Anne Scott recalled:

We used to go when there was still a mass of restrictions in force – in the 1950s you could take only £50 with you, for example, and I have never really understood why that was the case.

But the boat trains were always especially comfortable and very punctual – I think this was partly because a lot of people who travelled abroad in those days were either diplomats, or important business people or wealthy individuals. Boat trains didn't have Third Class passengers because people paying the lowest fares didn't travel abroad ever, unless they were servants accompanying their employers. So we all felt part of a rather privileged élite – a terrible thing to feel good about today I know, but things were so different then. One still felt sympathy for poorer people but no embarrassment about being well off oneself. I can remember watching crowds of people getting off a workmen's train that had just arrived at

'... in the 1950s you could only take £50 with you'

another platform while we waited in what I think was a luxurious Pullman carriage for our boat train to set off.

We holidayed one year in the Italian Lakes, and once on the Continent the trains seemed constantly to be changing engines, backing up and waiting; but when we went through that long pass under the Alps and emerged into sunlight and Italy, it really was heavenly, although we were told never to look out of the window because all the smuts from the engine would instantly fill your eyes if you did!

■ ORIGINALLY PHOTOGRAPHED FOR 'PICTURE POST', A COUPLE TAKE THE BOAT TRAIN ON THEIR WAY TO A HONEYMOON IN THE SOUTH OF FRANCE, MAY 1954.

The boat train service that started in the early 1950s and took passengers to and from Southampton Docks was remarkable in a number of ways, as Tom Shackle recalled:

Those trains were serving ships that took passengers across the Atlantic to New York, which was highly prestigious and attracted the seriously wealthy. To emphasize that this was a special service one or two of the engines were given suitable names – one was called Cunarder because the owner of the two most famous trans-Atlantic liners, the Queen Mary and the Queen Elizabeth, was the Cunard Shipping Line.

Those Cunard boat trains were initially beautifully fitted out – wonderfully clean and luxuriously decorated, and they continued to run from Waterloo to the docks until the end of trans-Atlantic passenger travel on ships. I believe that was right at the end of the 1960s, when the Queen Elizabeth and Queen Mary were decommissioned. By this time everyone was deserting the boats for aeroplanes.

■ THE BOAT TRAIN FROM SOUTHAMPTON ARRIVING AT WATERLOO STATION IN LONDON, 30TH MAY 1953. ON BOARD IS CROWN PRINCE AKIHITO OF JAPAN, WHO IS VISITING BRITAIN FOR THE CORONATION OF QUEEN ELIZABETH II.

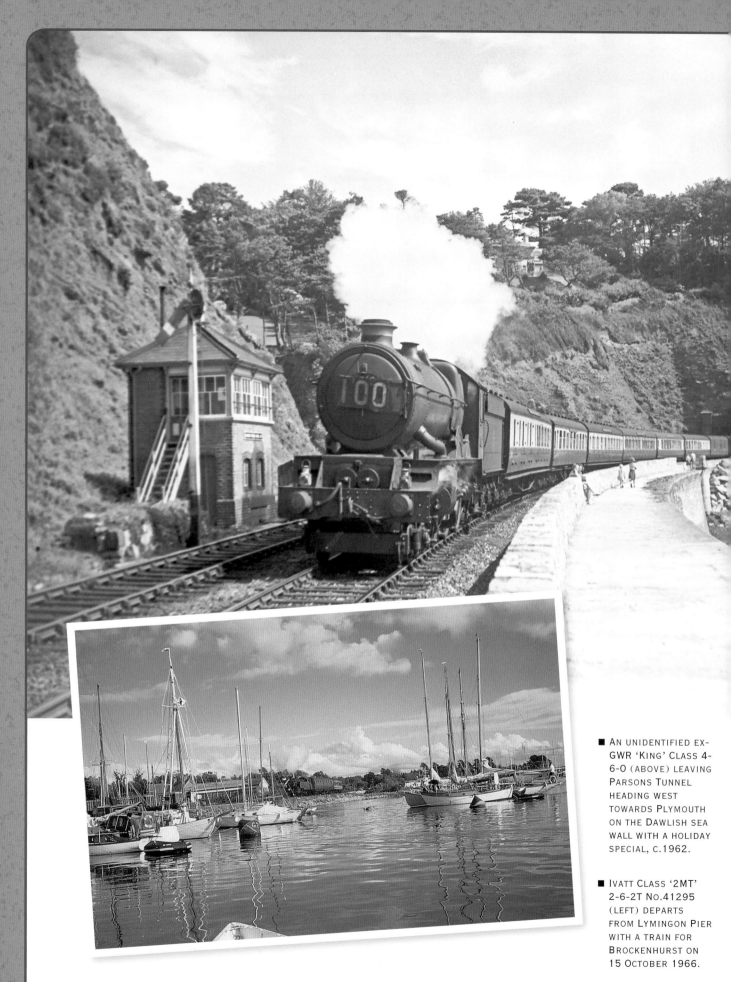

■ AN UNIDENTIFIED EX-GWR 'KING' CLASS 4-6-0 (ABOVE) LEAVING PARSONS TUNNEL HEADING WEST TOWARDS PLYMOUTH ON THE DAWLISH SEA WALL WITH A HOLIDAY SPECIAL, C.1962.

■ IVATT CLASS '2MT' 2-6-2T NO.41295 (LEFT) DEPARTS FROM LYMINGON PIER WITH A TRAIN FOR BROCKENHURST ON 15 OCTOBER 1966.

SCENIC ROUTES

Before motorways and sprawling housing estates, many railway journeys cut through otherwise unspoilt rural country that town-dwellers would not have experienced before. The bold engineering projects that carried rails high above deep valleys and along rugged coastlines made travelling by train a scenic treat.

■ THE 17.45 KYLE OF LOCHALSH TO INVERNESS TRAIN SKIRTS LOCH CARRON NEAR PLOCKTON IN JUNE 1958.

■ A STANIER CLASS '8F' 2-8-0 ABOUT TO PLUNGE INTO SUGAR LOAF TUNNEL WITH A NORTHBOUND FREIGHT FOR SHREWSBURY IN MAY 1964.

Overnight to the Hills – the Sleepers

Queen Victoria turned Scotland from a place of desolate landscapes and unyielding poverty into a region rich in romance and legend. She did for Scotland, if you like, what the Prince Regent did for Brighton – she transformed its fortunes.

But of course her interest and enthusiasm for Scotland was only really made possible by the railway and soon where Queen Victoria went the rich, and particularly the landed rich, were quick to follow, as Anne Scott recalled:

My whole family still went to Scotland on the sleeper when I was a child. My uncles took a house on the moors and we travelled north by train on August 10 or thereabouts so that my uncles and cousins could shoot grouse on the morning of the 12th. A lot of people we knew did the same and in fact in many years the whole train – or several trains – would be taken up by families who more or less knew one another. The social divisions were extraordinary, too, by today's standards. The family went in First Class, of course, and the servants in Third Class, with a special servant – perhaps the governess or nanny – sometimes in Second Class or even, if she were a much loved member of the family, in First Class; but that was very rare. What I remember best was the tea brought to one's berth and the astonishing sight of the mountains in the morning when one woke up. It was lovely!

■ A SCENE THAT WOULD NOT BE TOLERATED TODAY – PASSENGERS SMOKING IN A SLEEPING CAR IN THE 1930s.

'*What I remember most was the tea brought to one's berth*'

SLOW COACH
Queen Victoria frequently used the railway to travel long distances between her homes, Balmoral in Scotland and Osborne House on the Isle of Wight. The Queen's dislike of travelling fast imposed a speed limit of 40mph on the royal train, which proved very disruptive to normal rail traffic.

Guard John Kerley remembered the mountains of luggage: *The rich in summer – and in spring when they went north for the salmon fishing – turned up with lorry-loads of stuff all carried by servants who were helped by dozens of eager porters. They had pairs of guns in big leather cases, stacks of nets and fishing rods, baskets and dogs everywhere. The porters were enthusiastic because we all thought the posh really were better than the rest of us in those days, but also because we hoped for big tips; and sometimes the tips were very big. I can remember how shocked I was when a very grand Indian gentleman going north for the shooting gave me a tip that was virtually half a week's wages. I was never rude about foreigners again!*

But the old boys used to tell me about the days they remembered before the first war, when train after train left the station with just a few very rich families taking virtually every bed – now hardly anyone uses the sleepers because flying is so much quicker, and you can't blame them.

■ A CONVERTIBLE SLEEPER WITH TOP BERTH DOWN ON A BRITISH RAILWAYS SLEEPING CAR, 1965.

■ PASSENGERS (BELOW LEFT) COLLECTING FOOD TO EAT ON THE KING'S CROSS TO PERTH CAR-SLEEPER LIMITED IN JUNE 1955 – A SERVICE WHICH WAS WITHDRAWN IN 1988.

■ POSTCARD (BELOW RIGHT) ILLUSTRATING THE PLUSH SLEEPING CARS USED ON EAST COAST JOINT STOCK TRAINS BETWEEN LONDON AND EDINBURGH.

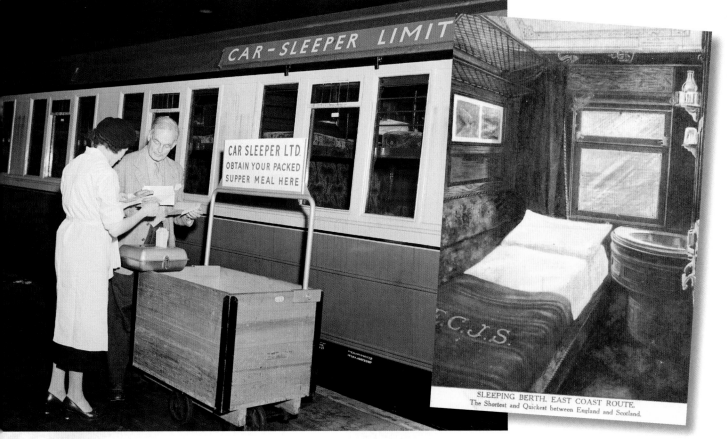

SLEEPING BERTH. EAST COAST ROUTE.
The Shortest and Quickest between England and Scotland.

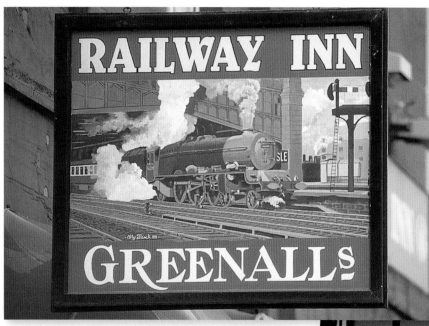

■ This railway inn sign (left) shows Stanier the 'Princess Royal' Class 4-6-2 No. 46200 leaving Carlisle Citadel station.

■ The Railway Inn at the south end of Dinmore Tunnel is about 7 1/2 miles north of Hereford (below left).

■ Bedlinog is an isolated village southeast of Merthyr Tydfil. This pub sign in the village (below) shows a GWR 56XX 0-6-2 tank locomotive, typical of the locomotives that once used the line through the village.

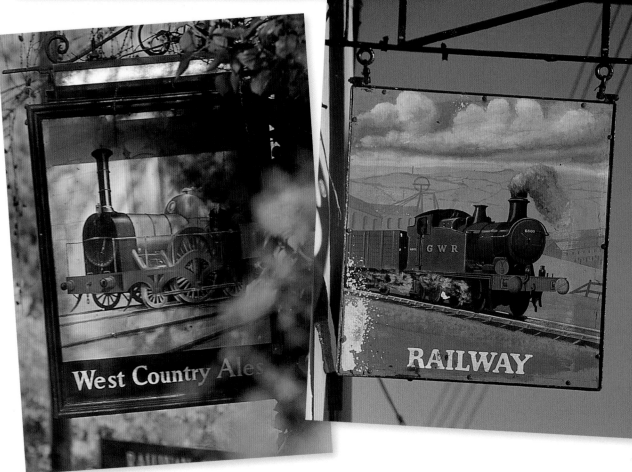

RAILWAY PUBS

Just as prominent landmarks had given their names to local inns and taverns down the centuries and 'The Coach and Horses' and names like it had commemorated a previous mode of transport, the coming of the railways gave birth to many new pubs and pub names. In some cases the pub name is the only remnant of a long abandoned line.

■ THE REQUEST STOP THAT INSPIRED THE NAMING OF THIS PUB IS AT LISS IN HAMPSHIRE ON THE MAIN LINE BETWEEN WATERLOO AND PORTSMOUTH.

■ AN INVENTIVE ILLUSTRATION FOR THE PUB SIGN ON BRIDGNORTH STATION PLATFORM ON THE PRESERVED SEVERN VALLEY RAILWAY.

■ THIS PUB, THAT BREWS ITS OWN BEER, OCCUPIES A BUILDING THAT WAS ORIGINALLY THE STATION HOTEL AT THE DEVON VILLAGE OF NEWTON ST CYRES.

■ THIS PUB IN STARCROSS, DEVON COMMEMORATES BRUNEL'S EXPERIMENT WITH ATMOSPHERIC PRESSURE-PROPELLED TRAINS. THE UNRELIABLE SYSTEM LASTED LESS THAN A YEAR, AFTER WHICH CONVENTIONAL STEAM LOCOMOTIVES PLIED THE SCENIC ROUTE BETWEEN EXETER AND NEWTON ABBOT.

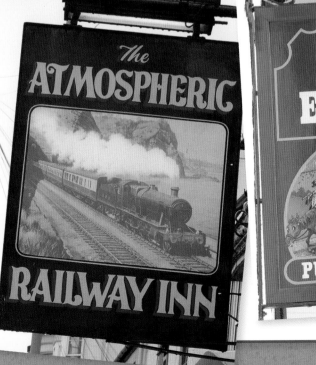

'... the carriages always seemed warm and comfortable to a ten-year-old boy!'

■ ISLE OF MAN RAILWAYS' 2-4-0T NO.8 'FENELLA', HAULING A PEEL TO DOUGLAS TRAIN ON 28 AUGUST 1967, IS ADMIRED AT ST JOHN'S BY A GROUP OF SCHOOLBOYS.

The Railway Islands

Despite their relatively small size, a number of Britain's off-shore islands had their own railways from quite early on, and those islands that were popular with holidaymakers often derived their popularity, in part at least, from their railways.

Martin Giles recalled childhood journeys on several different island railways in the 1950s:

One year we went to the Isle of Man, which was still very popular in the 1950s – unlike now, when the whole island is a bit of a ghost town unless you're a tax dodger with a case full of cash! Most of the old seaside boarding-houses and hotels look very shabby indeed but they didn't when I first visited. People used to get the boat from Liverpool and it felt like a foreign holiday. But best of all, we loved the little island railway that ran up past the Laxey Wheel – a huge watermill – into the hills above Douglas. This was, and still is I believe, a Victorian electric railway unspoiled by later developments and never changed; a sort of funicular with beautiful wooden seats in the carriages and that wonderful rattle of old wheels and loose windows.

Then there was the steam railway – still open and running today and never in fact closed down even when everywhere else steam had been abandoned. The Victorian engines and carriages used to carry us from Douglas through Port Soderick, Santon, Ballasalla, Castletown and Port St Mary to the southern resort of Port Erin. More than 15 miles of wonderful steam narrow gauge!

I remember the Old Isle of Wight steam railway too – we used to catch it from Ryde along to Newport, where my parents stayed in an old house each summer for a week and I used to walk out of town up the hill and along the River Medina to fish for mullet. The island steam railway was slow and dignified and the carriages always seemed warm and comfortable to a ten-year-old boy! Imagine, too, how much fun it was to get off the ferry from Portsmouth – that boat journey was a big excitement in itself – and then straight on to a wonderful steam train. I believe the trains still run on the island but I doubt if they are much fun now they're electric.

■ Ex-L&SWR Class '02' No.14 'Fishbourne' being serviced at Ryde St John's shed in October 1965. The Isle of Wight once boasted 56 miles of railways. Today, apart from the 5-mile Isle of Wight Steam Railway between Smallbrook Junction and Wootton, all that is left is the 8 1/2 mile electrified line between Ryde Pier Head and Shanklin.

■ Class '02' No.27 'Merstone' leaves Ryde Pier Head with a train for Cowes, 16 June 1964.

Index

Page numbers in **bold** refer to illustrations.

Picture Credits

DA Anderson © 168b

Ben Ashworth © 19m; 23r; 35t; 77t; 90tr; 91br; 121m; 121bl; 150bl; 151t; 167b; 170br; 171bl; 175tr; 178br; 179t; 180t; 180bl; 180br; 181t; 181bl; 181br; 197t; 204t; 205t; 206b; 207tr; 211tr; 221m; 225mr

Neil Baber © 36tl; 36bl; 141m; 141bl; 141br

British Rail © 114tl

HC Casserley © 113b

Derek Cross © 154b

Colour-Rail © 58b; 74bl; 87t; 91t; 93br; 95m; 96m; 97m; 99b; 115b; 118tr; 123tl; 153t; 156br; 157b; 159bl; 203b; 222/223; 236bl; 237mr; 237b

Kenneth Field © 40/41; 88b; 89b; 224b

John Goss © 32tl; 78t; 79m; 83t; 85b; 87b; 88t; 90br; 92t; 95b; 97t; 98b; 155t; 158bl; 158br; 159t; 159br; 161tl; 166b; 169t; 169b; 182bl; 183t; 188tr; 202t; 208tl; 208bl; 242t; 243t; 243b

Tony Harden © 25ml; 25mr; 43t; 66/67; 69m; 70tr; 74t; 93t; 102/103; 111t; 140tr; 174b; 187tl; 192t; 218t; 219tr; 226ml; 229bl; 230bl; 232tr; 232b; 239br

Tom Heavyside © 38t; 38bl; 38b; 70bl; 82m; 87m; 91bl; 150t; 152b; 155r; 158t; 176t; 178tl; 196b; 203t; 210tl; 211ml; 220t

Julian Holland © 39t; 39b; 68bl; 104m; 165t; 165b; 166t

Alan A Jackson © 110/111

Alan Jarvis © 60m; 61m; 212b

Getty Images © 16bl; 30tl; 31t; 31br; 30b; 34bl; 35b; 44t; 46t; 47t; 52bl; 54t; 63t; 64bl; 65bl; 71m; 100/101; 129bl; 130/131; 136b; 137t; 142m; 143t; 143br; 154t; 188b; 227b; 234t; 235t; 235b

Locomotive & General Photographs © 115t; 149b

Milepost © 14/15; 17m; 17tr; 18tl; 18bl; 19b; 20ml; 23b; 24b; 26/27; 28bl; 29tl; 29br; 31bl; 36br' 37tr; 37bl; 43b; 45t; 48m; 58t; 59b; 65t; 65br; 72m; 73tl; 75t; 76/77; 79tr; 80t; 80b; 81b; 84t; 84b; 85t; 85m; 94m; 95t; 98t; 103t; 104b; 105b; 107t; 107b; 108t; 109t; 109b; 113t; 116tl; 117t; 117b; 118tl; 120m; 120b; 121t; 121br; 122t; 123b; 124m; 125b; 128b; 129t; 129br; 138b; 139t; 140l; 140br; 141t; 144/145; 149m; 151b; 156tr; 157t; 161tr; 162tr; 162b; 163tl; 163b; 170bl; 171t; 171m; 171br; 175bl; 177b; 183b; 184tl; 184br; 185br; 189r; 192br; 193b; 194/195; 197b; 198t; 199t; 202bl; 202br; 203m;

205b; 209b; 210bl; 210br; 211br; 213t; 220b; 221t; 221br; 228mr; 229tr; 236t

Science & Society Photo Library © 20r; 21l; 21r; 22br; 33b; 42bl; 45b; 46b; 49b; 50tl; 50bl; 50/51; 51tr; 51br; 53t; 53b; 54b; 55tr; 55br; 56t; 56bl; 56br; 57tr; 57br; 62t; 65tr; 63b; 70tl; 70br; 110t; 110b; 120t; 132t; 133br; 134l; 137b; 160tr; 160bl; 161br; 187b; 188bl; 190bl; 191tl; 192bl; 193tr; 199m; 199b; 201t; 201b; 214t; 124bl; 215t; 215b; 217br; 230t; 230br; 231t; 231bl; 231br; 233t; 233b; 238bl; 239tr; 239bl

JR Smith © 90l; RFB Sniter © 90mr

Andrew Swift © 21b; 33t; 75m; 79b; 96b; 112b; 135b; 138tl; 186t; 186m; 186b; 187tr; 200b; 207tl; 216m; 219b; 225tr; 226b; 228b

TE Williams © 148t; 227t

Revd Graham Wise © 156bl

Acknowledgements

Over the past twenty-five years and more I have interviewed more than two hundred men and women who worked on the railways or travelled regularly by train in the days of steam. Their memories took me back, in some cases, as far as the pre-1914 railway.

I was remarkably lucky to have talked to them at a time when there was little interest among the general public in first-hand accounts of railway life, and I am grateful for their unfailing help and generosity. Sadly, most are now dead, but in many cases they became my friends and I hope that this book will stand in some sense as a memorial to their remarkable lives.

I'd also like to thank James Loader for his invaluable help, as well as the team at David and Charles: Julian Holland, Ali Myer, Neil Baber, Emily Pitcher, Sarah Clark and Sarah Wedlake.

Finally, for their enthusiasm for railways in general and for this book in particular I'd like to thank Alex, James, Katy, Charlotte and last but by no means least, Nutmeg.